W9-CBU-235

Greek and
Roman Sport

Titles in the World History Series

WORLD
HISTORY SERIES ■ ■ ■

Greek and Roman Sport

by Don Nardo

Lucent Books, P.O. Box 289011, San Diego, CA 92198-9011

Library of Congress Cataloging-in-Publication Data

Nardo, Don, 1947–
    Greek and Roman Sport / by Don Nardo.
       p. cm.—(World history series)
    Includes bibliographical references (p.   ) and index.
    Summary: Discusses the role of sports in the ancient
Greek and Roman World, covering the Olympics, the glories
of physical achievement, spectacle sports, horse and chariot
racing, and leisure sports.
    ISBN 1-56006-436-6   (lib. : alk. paper)
    1. Sports—Greece—History—Juvenile literature.
2. Sports—Rome—History—Juvenile literature.
[1. Sports—Greece—History.   2. Sports—Rome—History.]
I. Title. II. Series.
GV573.N37   1999
796'.0938—dc21   98–39636
                                              CIP
                                              AC

Copyright 1999 by Lucent Books, Inc., P.O. Box 289011,
San Diego, California 92198-9011

Printed in the U.S.A.

Contents

Foreword

Each year on the first day of school, nearly every history teacher faces the task of explaining why his or her students should study history. One logical answer to this question is that exploring what happened in our past explains how the things we often take for granted—our customs, ideas, and institutions—came to be. As statesman and historian Winston Churchill put it, "Every nation or group of nations has its own tale to tell. Knowledge of the trials and struggles is necessary to all who would comprehend the problems, perils, challenges, and opportunities which confront us today." Thus, a study of history puts modern ideas and institutions in perspective. For example, though the founders of the United States were talented and creative thinkers, they clearly did not invent the concept of democracy. Instead, they adapted some democratic ideas that had originated in ancient Greece and with which the Romans, the British, and others had experimented. An exploration of these cultures, then, reveals their very real connection to us through institutions that continue to shape our daily lives.

Another reason often given for studying history is the idea that lessons exist in the past from which contemporary societies can benefit and learn. This idea, although controversial, has always been an intriguing one for historians. Those who agree that society can benefit from the past often quote philosopher George Santayana's famous statement, "Those who cannot remember the past are condemned to repeat it." Historians who subscribe to Santayana's philosophy believe that, for example, studying the events that led up to the major world wars or other significant historical events would allow society to chart a different and more favorable course in the future.

Just as difficult as convincing students to realize the importance of studying history is the search for useful and interesting supplementary materials that present historical events in a context that can be easily understood. The volumes in Lucent Books' World History Series attempt to present a broad, balanced, and penetrating view of the march of history. Ancient Egypt's important wars and rulers, for example, are presented against the rich and colorful backdrop of Egyptian religious, social, and cultural developments. The series engages the reader by enhancing historical events with these cultural contexts. For example, in *Ancient Greece*, the text covers the role of women in that society. Slavery is discussed in *The Roman Empire*, as well as how slaves earned their freedom. The numerous and varied aspects of everyday life in these and other societies are explored in each volume of the series. Additionally, the series covers the major political, cultural, and philosophical ideas as the torch of civilization is passed from ancient Mesopotamia and Egypt, through Greece, Rome, Medieval Europe, and other world cultures, to the modern day.

The material in the series is formatted in a thorough, precise, and organized manner. Each volume offers the reader a comprehensive and clearly written overview of an important historical event or period. The topic under discussion is placed in a broad historical context. For example, *The Italian Renaissance* begins with a discussion of the High Middle Ages and the loss of central control that allowed certain Italian cities to develop artistically. The book ends by looking forward to the Reformation and interpreting the societal changes that grew out of the Renaissance. Thus, students are not only involved in an historical era, but also enveloped by the events leading up to that era and the events following it.

One important and unique feature in the World History Series is the primary and secondary source quotations that richly supplement each volume. These quotes are useful in a number of ways. First, they allow students access to sources they would not normally be exposed to because of the difficulty and obscurity of the original source. The quotations range from interesting anecdotes to farsighted cultural perspectives and are drawn from historical witnesses both past and present. Second, the quotes demonstrate how and where historians themselves derive their information on the past as they strive to reach a consensus on historical events. Lastly, all of the quotes are footnoted, familiarizing students with the citation process and allowing them to verify quotes and/or look up the original source if the quote piques their interest.

Finally, the books in the World History Series provide a detailed launching point for further research. Each book contains a bibliography specifically geared toward student research. A second, annotated bibliography introduces students to all the sources the author consulted when compiling the book. A chronology of important dates gives students an overview, at a glance, of the topic covered. Where applicable, a glossary of terms is included.

In short, the series is designed not only to acquaint readers with the basics of history, but also to make them aware that their lives are a part of an ongoing human saga. Perhaps they will then come to the same realization as famed historian Arnold Toynbee. In his monumental work, *A Study of History*, he wrote about becoming aware of history flowing through him in a mighty current, and of his own life "welling like a wave in the flow of this vast tide."

Important Dates in the History of Greek and Roman Sport

B.C. ca. 1200 776 753 724 708 680 540–516 520 490 480 420 396 164–152 65 2 A.D. 80

B.C.

ca. 1200
Date of the legendary Trojan War, subject of the Greek poet Homer's *Iliad*, the first known example of Western literature that contains descriptions of chariot races and other athletic events.

776
Traditional date for the first Olympic Games, held thereafter every four years at the religious sanctuary at Olympia in southwestern Greece. At first, the program consists of just one event, a short footrace. Sometime shortly before or after this date, Homer composes the *Iliad* and its sequel, the *Odyssey*.

753
According to later Roman scholars, the year that the legendary figure Romulus founded the city of Rome. Supposedly he held chariot races shortly afterward.

724
The Greeks add a second footrace to the Olympic program.

708
The pentathlon, consisting of five events, including the discus throw and wrestling, becomes part of the program at Olympia.

680
The Olympics begin to feature a four-horse chariot race.

540–516
Milo of Kroton, perhaps the greatest wrestler of all time, wins the wrestling competition in six separate Olympiads.

520
A footrace in which the runners are clad in armor and carry a shield becomes part of the Olympic program.

490
The Athenians defeat an invading Persian army in the Battle of Marathon; afterward, according to legend, an Athenian soldier runs over twenty-five miles to Athens to announce the victory and dies of exhaustion; more than two thousand years later, this tale inspires the creation of the modern marathon event.

480
The Greeks defeat the Persians in a great naval battle in the bay of Salamis, southwest of Athens. This engagement is later frequently recreated in naval battles staged as entertainment by Roman emperors.

420
Sparta is excluded from the current session of the Olympic Games for breaking the sacred Olympic truce, which forbids making war during the season in which the games are held.

396
Kyniska, daughter of a Greek aristocrat, wins the Olympic prize when her chariot team achieves victory; she wins again in 392.

164–152
A runner named Leonidas of Rhodes wins all three major footraces in four successive Olympiads, a feat unprecedented in ancient times.

65
The Roman politician Julius Caesar presents 320 pairs of gladiators in games he stages in Rome.

2

The first Roman emperor, Augustus, entertains his subjects with a spectacular naval battle staged in a specially dug artificial lake.

A.D.

80

The emperor Titus inaugurates Rome's new amphitheater, the Colosseum, with games in which some nine thousand animals are slaughtered.

107

Trajan, another Roman emperor, stages games in which thousands of gladiators fight and over eleven thousand beasts meet their doom.

ca. 150–175

The Greek traveler Pausanias writes his *Guide to Greece*, which contains the most detailed descriptions of ancient Greek athletic sites, including the one at Olympia.

393

The Christian emperor Theodosius I bans all pagan (non-Christian) religions, possibly ending the Olympics and other Greek festivals featuring athletic competitions.

ca. 440

The last gladiatorial fights are held in Rome.

476

In the wake of repeated invasions by northern European peoples, the last western Roman emperor is forced from his throne.

532

Rivalry among chariot-racing factions and fans in Constantinople, formerly the Roman Empire's eastern capital, leads to rioting, arson, and the slaughter of over thirty thousand people in the city's racetrack.

1453

The Ottoman Turks capture Constantinople, eradicating the last surviving remnant of classical (ancient Greek and Roman) civilization.

1766

The site of ancient Olympia, long lost to the world, is rediscovered.

1859 and 1870

The Greek government stages local athletic contests in Athens in an attempt to revive the ancient Olympics.

1896

The first modern international Olympic Games, organized by French aristocrat Pierre de Coubertin, are held in Athens.

1912

Jim Thorpe, an American Indian, wins the Olympic decathlon and pentathlon in Stockholm, Sweden; soon afterward, Olympic officials charge him with professionalism and take back his medals.

1959

MGM releases a film version of Lew Wallace's novel *Ben-Hur*, which features an elaborate and exciting depiction of ancient Roman chariot racing.

2004

The modern Olympic Games return to Athens, Greece.

Those of Whom the Poets Sing

The simple and convenient modern word *sports* collectively describes many and diverse kinds of athletic competitions and leisure activities, from hunting and fishing to football, horse racing, and discus throwing. The ancient Greeks and Romans had no such all-encompassing word to describe these activities, all of which they engaged in. As a rule, they referred to each, as well as to various other physical games and spectacles that we would loosely define as sports, separately. Yet it should not be interpreted from their lack of a collective word for sports that such activities were of minor importance to them; in fact, just the opposite is true. For large numbers of Greeks and Romans, either taking part in or watching sports was an integral part of life. For the Greeks in particular, sports were not only immensely popular physical and leisure activities but also serious subjects for intellectuals and artists. Classical scholar David Sansone explains:

> What is remarkable about Greek sport is the seriousness with which it was taken as a cultural and even religious phenomenon. Serious writers and thinkers in ancient Rome tended to scorn the Circus and avoid the arena, just as intellectuals today despise, or affect to despise, popular sport. But in

ancient Greece the story was different. It is not unusual for a dramatist like Aeschylus [fifth century B.C.] to draw his metaphors, or for a philosopher like Plato [fourth century B.C.] to select his illustrations, from the realms of chariot racing or wrestling. Indeed, in the hands of the most distinguished [Greek] poets and artists, sport becomes itself the subject of great art. Everyone is familiar, for example, with Myron's statue of a discus-thrower.[1]

Early Rituals and Royal Hunts

Despite the great popularity and importance of sports in the Greek and Roman world, as well as in modern society, scholars are still unsure of how and when sports began. Some experts suggest that they grew out of the biological need and impulse to play, an activity that enables people (and animals) to learn from interacting with their surroundings and experimenting with the physical potential of their own bodies. Other scholars think that sports developed from activities connected with various religious, social, and/or survival rituals that became long-standing tra-

The Discobulus, or "Discus Thrower," by the fifth-century B.C. sculptor Myron, is one of the most famous statues ever created. This is a marble copy of the original bronze, which was lost in antiquity (ancient times).

spectators is the release of energy involved in the ritual. The person who releases the most energy—that is, the one who throws the farthest or runs the fastest—becomes the most honored.[3]

Whatever the physical and psychological reasons why humans began engaging in sportlike activities, all scholars agree that such activities long predated Greek civilization. At least as early as the second millennium B.C., ancient Mesopotamian and Egyptian rulers and aristocrats staged elaborate hunts in chariots. Although not formal competitions, the hunters no doubt displayed a competitive spirit since the person who killed the most or biggest animals received the most adulation. In time spectators apparently watched these events as well as others in which a king or noble performed various feats from a moving chariot. An Egyptian painting shows the pharaoh Amenophis II (fifteenth century B.C.) shooting at a target while driving a chariot. The inscription reads: "His Majesty performed these feats before the eyes of the whole land."[4] Perhaps such events can be thought of as the distant forerunners of Greek and Roman chariot races. Mesopotamian and Egyptian reliefs also show men wrestling and swimming; however, these appear to have been informal and individual activities rather than organized competitions.[5]

ditions. Sansone gives the example of ancient and modern javelin throwers. "The participants," he says, "are throwing the javelin because men in the previous generation threw the javelin, and in the generation before that . . . and so on back to a time when there was in fact a connection between javelin-throwing and hunting."[2] In this view, the original need or meaning of the activity is lost over time, and what remains important for the participants and

Mind and Body

All available evidence suggests that formal, organized sports contests in the modern sense originated in ancient Greece. At least by the early Archaic Age (ca. 800–500 B.C.) and probably a good deal earlier, the

Egyptian royal hunts, like the one depicted in this wall painting of the Pharaoh Amenophis II, may have been early forerunners of Greek and Roman chariot races.

Greeks used the word *agon*, meaning contest or struggle, to describe athletic contests (as well as other kinds of contests, such as battles and lawsuits). And it was in this period, in 776 B.C. to be exact, that, according to Greek tradition, the first Olympic Games were held. It was also in early Archaic times, or slightly before, that the famous poet Homer composed the two long poems that became Greece's treasured national epics—the *Iliad* (the story of the Trojan War) and the *Odyssey* (the adventures of the Greek hero Odysseus in the years following the war). These works contain the world's first literary descriptions of

sports competitions. In the *Iliad*, for instance, the Greek hero Achilles organizes games, including a chariot race, in honor of his recently slain friend, Patroclus. Homer describes the race's exciting start:

They were all off together at once, whipping up the horses, flicking them with the reins, crying them on furiously. The ships were left behind, and away they galloped—their manes went flying on the wind and clouds of dust rose under their bodies. The chariots now ran steady, now bounded high; the drivers stood on their platforms with hearts beating high in hope. Every man called to his horses, and the horses flew over the ground.[6]

It is possible that Greeks in the age of the Trojan War (ca. 1200 B.C.) held such races and that Homer merely repeated old accounts of them. But more probably, even if such races did take place that far back, he was describing versions from his own time. His detailed and dramatic account of the race, historian Vera Olivova suggests, was less likely a "reflection of a centuries-old tradition" and more likely "an eyewitness

account, by one who had ample opportunity to witness such races."[7]

Wherever Homer's inspirations came from, what is certain is that in the two centuries following his time athletic competitions became increasingly popular throughout the Greek world. And a new, uniquely Greek concept emerged—*kalokagathia* (from the words *kalos*, meaning "beautiful," and *agathos*, meaning "noble" or "learned"). This concept translates roughly as the "mind-body ideal." At first fashionable mainly in aristocratic circles but later popular with Greeks of other

Odysseus Wins the Silver Bowl

In this excerpt from book 23 of Homer's Iliad *(W. H. D. Rouse's translation), the wily Odysseus, with a little help from a friendly goddess, wins the footrace staged by Achilles to honor the dead Patroclus.*

"Achilles now brought out prizes for the footrace. There was a silver mixing-bowl finely wrought. . . the most beautiful bowl in the world. . . . 'Rise any who wish to run for this prize,' [Achilles declared]. Aias the runner rose, Odysseus rose, then Nestor's son, Antilochos, for he was the best runner among the young men. . . . The pace was forced from the start, but before long Aias was leading with Odysseus close behind him. . . . Odysseus trod in his [Aias's] footsteps before the dust had time to settle, and the breath of Odysseus beat on his head as he ran; the spectators cheered his efforts, but he was doing his very best already. When they came to the last bit of course Odysseus offered a silent prayer to Athena. 'Hear me, my goddess, give your good help to my feet!' Pallas Athena heard and made his limbs light. . . . And when they [the runners] were just about to pounce on the prize, Athena tripped Aias and made him slip. . . . So Odysseus came in first and [in triumph] lifted the mixing-bowl. . . . [Aias complained] 'Damn it, that goddess tripped me up! She's always by his side like a mother and helps him!' All present burst into a roar of laughter."

classes, *kalokagathia* stressed striving for a combination of physical and mental excellence to develop a rounded and complete personality. Thus, many Greeks came to glorify a keen mind in a strong, athletic body. Just how deeply this notion became ingrained in the popular consciousness is illustrated by a common ancient Greek proverb describing a backward person: "He can neither read nor swim."[8] Though not every Greek man and woman was physically and mentally equipped to achieve the mind-body ideal, the fact that so many wanted and tried to achieve it influenced the development of Greek customs and institutions. In Greece's Classic Age (ca. 500–300 B.C.) athletic training and sports contests became common facets of everyday life; and the gymnasium, in which patrons received both physical and academic training, became an obligatory facility in every Greek city-state.

The Life Span of Classical Sports

Later the Romans, who conquered Greece (in the second century B.C.) and adopted many aspects of Greek culture, created their own sports competitions and institutions. The major difference was that Rome's most popular games, gladiatorial combats and chariot races, were much more violent and/or larger in scale than Greek athletic contests, which continued to be held under Roman rule. Unlike Greek wrestlers and boxers, for example, Roman gladiators routinely fought to the death. And Roman charioteers competed in huge stone facilities seating tens or even hundreds of thousands of spectators, as compared to their Greek counterparts who raced mostly in open fields.

An artist's conception of the complex of sports facilities, temples, and treasuries at Olympia as it likely appeared in Greece's Classic Age.

Generally speaking, the development and life span of these ancient Greco-Roman, or classical, sports was rather neatly encompassed by the life span of the Olympic Games, held every four years at Olympia in southwestern Greece. The inception of these most prestigious of all ancient games in the 700s B.C. marked the effective beginning of classical sports; and the shutdown of Olympia's facilities (roughly coinciding with the banning of gladiatorial fights throughout the Roman Empire) in the late A.D 300s, shortly before Rome's fall, marked their effective end.[9] Thus, Greco-Roman sports were popular and thriving activities for almost twelve centuries.

Thanks to the survival of various forms of ancient evidence, modern scholars have been able to piece together a fairly accurate reconstruction of the development and staging of many of the sporting events of these centuries. First, archaeological studies of the remains of ancient stadiums, arenas, gymnasiums, and the like are a vital source of information about ancient sports. Also, the large Greek national festivals that featured sports contests, including the one held regularly at Olympia, kept records of winners, events, and dates. These records have not survived intact, but fortunately sections of them were quoted by later ancient authors whose works have survived. Sports scenes painted on pottery or carved into stone comprise still another important source of information, as do various surviving examples of ancient literature. These forms of expression, especially poetry written about contests and athletes, constituted in a sense the popular sports media of their time. Among the most important ancient writers about sports and games, after Homer, were the brilliant Greek poet Pindar (fifth century

A bust of Pindar (Pindaros in Greek), the fifth-century B.C. lyric poet who wrote odes to Olympic victors.

B.C.), who wrote odes honoring Olympic winners; the Greek traveler Pausanias (second century A.D.), who wrote the world's first known guidebook; and the Greek physician Galen (second century A.D.), whose works provide valuable information about athletes' and gladiators' training, diet, and injuries.

Of these and the other ancient writers who recorded sports lore, Pindar best captured the competitive spirit of the participants, the burning desire to win, and the high degree of personal glory that winning brought. "That man is happy and poets sing of him," Pindar writes, "who conquers with hand or swift foot and wins the greatest of prizes by steadfastness and strength, and lives to see his young son, in turn, get garlands [victory wreaths]."[10] These are some of the same qualities that characterize popular sports today, when top athletes are still praised by the media and idolized as heroes.

1 For the Honor of Zeus: The Great Olympic Festival and Games

The ancient Olympics purportedly began in 776 B.C. Now viewed as the formal beginning of Greco-Roman sports, they were the most famous, prestigious, and long-lasting of all ancient games. But they were not the only Greek athletic competitions. Many others developed over the years, all of them, like the Olympics that served as their model, connected to various religious ceremonies honoring the gods. Each Greek city-state, or polis, had a special open-air space where sacred rituals took place. Eventually temples, at first made of wood and later of stone, rose in these spaces, called sanctuaries.

During religious festivals at the sanctuaries, worshipers marched in formal processions, performed sacrifices of plants and animals, and staged musical and athletic contests. The musical *agon* (contest) often consisted of competitions on various musical instruments and poetry recitations; the athletic *agon* eventually included several running, jumping, and throwing

This scene from a fifth-century B.C. tablet found at Corinth shows worshipers preparing to perform sacrifices. The person at left carries a phiale, *a container bearing liquid offerings.*

events that are today termed "track-and-field," along with wrestling, boxing, and horse and chariot racing. In all of these sacred contests, the participants dedicated their creative or physical skills and prowess to the local sanctuary's god or gods. Thus, an early hymn to Apollo (god of sporting events as well as light and healing) describes ceremonies in which "the Greeks gather in long chitons [tunics], together with their children and respectful women, to pay you honor. Every contest they organize is for your delight: boxing and dancing and singing."[11]

In time hundreds of local sacred games were held across the Greek world.[12] But by the end of the sixth century B.C., four of these had emerged as preeminent. They were not only the most prestigious such events, but they were also international rather than local in character, drawing competitors and spectators from city-states far and wide. The greatest of all, of course, was the Olympic festival (honoring Zeus, leader of the gods), held at Olympia in southwestern Greece every four years. The others included the Pythian Games (honoring Apollo), held the third year after each Olympics at the sacred shrine at Delphi in central Greece; the Isthmian Games (honoring Poseidon, god of the seas), staged every two years at a sanctuary on the Isthmus of Corinth, the narrow land bridge connecting southern and central Greece; and the Nemean Games (also honoring Zeus), held at two-year intervals at Nemea, a few miles south of Corinth.

Together these "big four" festivals, in which sports contests became by far the chief attraction, made up the so-called *periodos*, or "circuit" (also known as the Crown Games or Period Games). Another highly

The Greek World

popular and prestigious festival was the Panathenaea (meaning "all the Athenians"), held at Athens, the most populous Greek city, every four years in honor of Athena, goddess of wisdom and war. Because these events drew people from all across the Greek world, they were termed *panhellenic*, or "all-Greek."[13] Although the city-states saw themselves as tiny separate nations, these events, like the Greek language and the worship of Zeus, Apollo, and the other Olympian gods, served to bind all Greeks together. As Vera Olivova writes,

The sites of the four main games . . . became focal points for the whole Greek world. Amid the fertile variety of the city-states, free of pressure from any central power, it was here that a sense of national identity arose in a purely natural and spontaneous way, through awareness of a high level of shared culture both intellectual and physical, and through a sense of superiority over the slaves and over the neighboring barbarians [the term the

Greeks used to describe non-Greek-speaking peoples]. The outward symbol of this superiority was a strong, tanned, well-developed naked body. It became an ideal for all Greeks, distinguishing them from other peoples, and an object of admiration at all panhellenic festivals.[14]

Generally speaking, the same events and customs practiced at Olympia, Delphi, and the other circuit sites prevailed at other games, only on a smaller scale. Therefore, an examination of the famous festival and games at Olympia gives a reasonably comprehensive and accurate picture of ancient Greek athletics.

Origins in the Mists of Time

Ancient Olympia was located in a picturesque rural region of the northwestern Peloponnesus (the large peninsula that makes up the southern third of Greece). The sanctuary, consisting of temples, shrines, and sports facilities, rested along the banks of the Alpheus River within the territory of the polis of Elis. According to legend, the semidivine hero Heracles (whom the Romans called Hercules) performed twelve superhuman labors, one of which was cleaning the vast cattle stables of King Augeas of Elis. To celebrate this feat, Heracles supposedly single-handedly created Olympia's sacred grove and instituted its first games in honor of Zeus, his father. Because Zeus was the chief Olympian, the games became known, appropriately, as the Olympics.

The reality is that no one knows when Olympia's religious festivals and their attendant games began. Archaeology has shown that the site was inhabited as far back as the third millennium B.C., early in Greece's Bronze Age (ca. 3000–1150 B.C., the era the classical Greeks called the Age of Heroes) and that some kind of religious ceremonies took place there from that time on. The identities of the original gods worshiped at the sanctuary are lost in the mists of time; but even after Zeus became the main and permanent focus of worship there, shrines remained honoring various nature gods and also the local hero Pelops, after whom the Peloponnesus was named. There is little doubt that sports contests were held at Olympia well before the traditional starting date of 776 B.C. But that date, when the athlete Coroebus of Elis was crowned the first Olympic victor, apparently marks the beginning of the games' ongoing four-year cycle and the systematic recording of winners.

One might well ask how a local festival in a backward farming region rose to such prominence in the Greek world. At least part of the answer, noted scholars M. I. Finley and H. W. Pleket suggest, was Elis's very unimportance:

> Games everywhere were managed by local authorities, not by an international committee, and the weaker that authority the less risk that the prestige of a great festival would enhance its political power. Athletes from all over the Greek world could safely compete for their own glory and that of their own cities, without building up the prestige of a powerful host-community.[15]

Yet while Elis remained a politically and militarily weak city-state, its authority over the Olympic festival was considerable. The *Hellanodikai*, or Hellenic judges, who exercised strict control over the contests and whose decisions were final, were

Digging Up Ancient Olympia

This excerpt from The Cambridge Illustrated History of Archaeology *describes modern excavations of the site of Olympia, including the recent discovery of a cup that might have belonged to one of the ancient world's most famous individuals.*

"Olympia in the western Peloponnesus attracted early interest from German excavators, who began work in the 1870s. This cult center dedicated to Zeus, the chief deity of the Greeks, had as its focus a huge colonnaded temple measuring 28 by 64 meters (92 by 210 feet) which from the fifth century B.C. contained Phidias's monumental statue of the god. Digging through a layer of silt left by medieval flooding, the team discovered the substructure of the temple complete, its columns toppled by earthquakes. Amid the debris lay the pedimental sculptures described by Pausanias: vivid depictions of the mythological foundation of the Olympic Games. . . . Relief sculptures in the metopes [rectangular panels running along the temple's sides] depicted the labors of Heracles. Further excavations have since revealed the temple of Hera, the consort of Zeus, the treasuries for individual Greek states, and the classical Olympic stadium—a linear running track one *stadion* (192.28 meters or 630 feet) long, set between parallel earthen banks that provided seating for spectators. The long tradition of excavating at Olympia has brought more recent finds too. Pausanias mentions the workshop in which the huge gold and ivory statue of Zeus was created by the sculptor Phidias. . . . Excavations have discovered both the workshop and debris that includes a mug with the supposedly ancient inscription 'I belong to Phidias.'"

The ruins of Olympia, some of which are shown here, remained largely buried by silt for many centuries.

Eleans. Originally there were two of these men, probably Elean nobles, who combined the jobs of general games organizer, supervisor of training, and umpire of events. By the early fifth century B.C. the number of judges had increased to ten, by then selected by popular vote and the drawing of lots. They were unpaid and wore special purple robes, symbolic of their high status.[16] The degree of their prestige and authority is attested by the penalties they could and sometimes did mete out for such acts as cheating or bribery, including fines,[17] exclusion from the games, and even public flogging.

The judges' broad powers, combined with the fact that their fellow Eleans regularly competed in the games, occasionally brought into question their fairness and impartiality. In the games of 396 B.C., for example, two of the three judges overseeing the running events were severely criticized when they awarded victory in a hotly contested footrace to an Elean runner over a rival from another polis. The fifth-century B.C. Greek historian Herodotus told a legendary story about how, in the dim past, a group of Eleans journeyed to Egypt and bragged about how fairly they ran the Olympics. Egyptian leaders asked the visitors if Eleans were allowed to compete in the games and hearing that they were,

> expressed the opinion that to organize the games on such a principle was not fair at all; for it was quite impossible, when men from one's own city took part in some event, not to favor them at the expense of the strangers. If they really wanted to play fair at the games . . . they should open the various events to visitors only, and not allow anyone from Elis to compete.[18]

Whether or not this story is true (it certainly smacks of fable), the Eleans remained eligible in the Olympic contests. Yet flagrant favoritism by the Elean judges was probably rare, for otherwise the games at Olympia would not have retained so exalted a reputation for so many centuries.

The Sacred Truce, the Facilities, and the Crowds

Another of Elis's duties in organizing the games every four years consisted of announcing them to the Greek world. Three Elean heralds, the *spondophoroi*, or truce-bearers, wearing olive wreaths and carrying staffs, visited every Greek state. Their job was to tell the exact date of the coming games (which varied from one Olympiad to the next), to invite all to attend, and, most important of all, to announce the sacred Olympic truce, or *ekecheiria*. During this truce, originally a month and later extended to three months, all participating states were forbidden from making war or imposing death penalties. This was to ensure safe passage for the thousands of competitors, spectators, and religious pilgrims who attended the games. Violators were severely penalized. In 420 B.C., for instance, Sparta, the famous militaristic polis located in the southern Peloponnesus, was excluded from the Olympics and heavily fined for breaking the truce. And in the following century Macedonia's king Alexander (later called "the Great") was obliged to pay damages to an Athenian pilgrim who had been robbed en route to Olympia by some of the renowned general's troops.

Upon reaching Olympia, such travelers were greeted with an impressive array

Phidias's monumental statue of Zeus rests in the god's temple at Olympia in this modern reconstruction based on Pausanias's description. The Olympic Zeus was later designated as one of the seven wonders of the ancient world.

of buildings, shrines, and athletic facilities. By the second century B.C. these included Zeus's great altar, where the principal sacrifices took place, and temples dedicated to Zeus, Hera (Zeus's wife and protector of marriage), and Rhea (Zeus's mother). The Temple of Zeus contained a huge statue of the god, made in the fifth century B.C. by Phidias, now recognized as the greatest sculptor of the ancient world. Pausanias's famous second-century A.D. guidebook provides the following eyewitness account of this magnificent creation, the ancient world's most highly venerated statue, which was unfortunately destroyed or lost in subsequent centuries:

It was Phidias who made the statue, as an inscription written below Zeus's feet bears witness: "Phidias, the son of Charmides from Athens, has made me.". . . The god is sitting on a throne; he is made of gold and ivory. There is a wreath on his head like twigs and leaves of olive; in his right hand he is holding a [smaller statue of the goddess] Victory of gold and ivory with a ribbon and a wreath on her head; in the god's left hand is a staff in blossom with every kind of precious metal, and the bird perching on this staff is Zeus's eagle [one of his symbols; the thunderbolt was another]. The god's sandals are gold and so is his cloak. . . . The throne is finely worked with gold and gems, and with ebony and with ivory. There are animals painted on it and figures sculpted on it. . . . On the topmost part of the throne above the statue's head Phidias has carved three Graces and three Seasons. Epic poetry tells us they were among Zeus's daughters, and Homer has written in the *Iliad* that the Seasons were given charge of heaven like some kind of royal palace guards. . . . On the platform that holds up Zeus and all the decoration that goes with him there are golden figures of the Sun [i.e., the god Helios] mounting his chariot, and Zeus and Hera . . . followed by Hermes. . . . [It is said that] the god himself bore witness to the art of Phidias: when the statue was completely finished, Phidias prayed to the god to make a sign if the work pleased him, and immediately a flash of lightning struck the pavement.[19]

The Olympic sanctuary also featured eleven treasuries (storehouses for gold and other offerings to the gods) fashioned to look like miniature temples, a stadium for track-and-field events, a hippodrome for horse and chariot races, a gymnasium, public baths, and numerous other buildings, altars, shrines, and statues.

One Olympic building, the Leonidaion (built in the fourth century B.C. from funds donated by a well-to-do individual from the Aegean island of Naxos), was a hotel used by important officials, visiting royalty, and a few athletes and trainers. The site's only substantial lodging, this and the on-site baths could not begin to accommodate the gigantic crowds that attended the games. These included not only the athletes, trainers, and spectators but also singers, dancers, orators, fast-food sellers and other merchants, gamblers and con men, and pimps and prostitutes (who operated outside the sanctuary since women were excluded from watching as well as competing in the games). Most of the estimated fifty to sixty thousand or more visitors slept in tents or under the stars and had to cart their own water from springs inconveniently located almost a kilometer (approximately half a mile) north of the sanctuary.[20] The thousands of people and animals raised a lot of dust, and the temperature in August, when the games took place, averaged close to ninety degrees Fahrenheit (about thirty-two degrees Celsius). A descriptive passage by the first-century A.D. philosopher Epictetus gives some idea of the uncomfortable conditions and also suggests why so many were willing to put up with them:

> There are enough irksome and troublesome things in life; aren't things just as bad at the Olympic festival? Aren't you scorched there by the fierce heat? Aren't you crushed in the crowd? Isn't it difficult to freshen yourself up? Doesn't the rain soak you to the skin? Aren't you bothered by the noise, the din and other nuisances? But it seems to me that you are well able to bear and indeed gladly endure all this, when you think of the gripping spectacles that you will see.[21]

The Olympic Program

The exact schedule and sequence of these "spectacles," which consistently attracted large crowds for some twelve centuries, remain unknown. But available evidence suggests that the following reconstruction is the most plausible (after the games were reorganized in the early fifth century B.C.). During the summer of an Olympic year, the athletes were required to arrive in Elis at least a month early and to train under the watchful eye of Elean officials. Two days before the opening of the games, the competitors, trainers, and judges marched the thirty-six miles from Elis to Olympia along a road known as the Sacred Way. Simultaneously, tens of thousands of spectators and others converged on the site from all directions.

The actual Olympic program took place over a five-day period. The first day witnessed the swearing-in ceremony in a building called the Bouleuterion (Council Chamber), located about fifty meters (fifty-five yards) south of the great Temple of Zeus. According to Pausanias, oaths were sworn before a statue of Zeus:

> The tradition dictates that the athletes and their fathers and brothers and even their trainers should take before this statue an oath . . . to do no wrong to the Olympic Games. The actual athletes have to swear further

Pilgrims from many Greek states make their way toward the Olympic sanctuary in Elis, in the northwestern reaches of the Peloponnesus.

A sacrificial offering at the Temple of Apollo at Delphi, in central Greece, home of the Pythian Games. Religious ceremonies like this one were common at the Olympic, Nemean, and other major festival sites.

that they have been in full training for ten months.[22]

In addition, Pausanias informs us, the judges swore to be fair, not to take bribes, and to keep secret anything they had learned about the athletes during the training period. The rest of the first day was devoted to private and public prayers, public sacrifices, the consulting of oracles (priestesses thought to act as mediums between gods and humans), and orations by philosophers, historians, and others. In short, day one at the Olympic festival was mainly ceremonial in nature.

The schedule of the other four days was quite varied. The horse and chariot races were held in the hippodrome in the morning of day two; the pentathlon (combination of running, jumping, discus throw, javelin throw, and wrestling) took place in the afternoon; and the evening was devoted to funeral rites for the hero Pelops, communal singing of victory hymns, and feasting. Day three (calculated to coincide with the full moon) was the most religious day of the festival. In the morning, a great procession marched to Zeus's outdoor altar (located about sixty meters, or sixty-six yards, north of the god's temple) and there sacrificed one hundred oxen. "The first step of the altar," Pausanias writes,

is 125 feet in circumference and is called the "Outer Circle." The step above the Outer Circle is 32 feet in circumference. The total height of the altar is 22 feet. The rule is to kill the animals in the lower part of the Outer Circle and then to carry the thighs to the top of the altar and burn them there as a scarifice.[23]

In the afternoon, following these sacrifices, the boys' competitions (for youths between the ages of twelve and eighteen) were held, and that evening saw a lavish banquet in which the flesh of the slain oxen was consumed. Day four was devoted to the footraces and the combat sports (wrestling, boxing, and the *pankration*, a rough and tumble form of both). Finally, on the fifth day the victors were crowned and there were more sacrifices, feasts, and other celebrations.

Women Athletes and Spectators

After the religious ceremonies, the athletes were, of course, the main focus of attention throughout the entire five-day festival. At first only free males could compete in the Olympic or any other athletic competition.[24] Women and slaves could not take part and women could not even watch, although there were exceptions to this rule. A priestess of Demeter (a fertility goddess) was actually expected to witness the Olympic contests, for example.

Over time women across the Greek and Roman world demanded that they be allowed to participate. And by the first century B.C. the Pythian, Isthmian, and

A priestess of Demeter, the goddess who presided over agriculture, sits in a special set of box seats overlooking the Olympic stadium. Such priestesses were a rare exception to the rule prohibiting women from watching the contests.

Nemean Games, along with many local games, not only admitted women as spectators but also allowed them to compete in a few "ladies only" events. In addition a small separate women's contest was held at Olympia every four years—the Heraea, honoring the goddess Hera. Sixteen Elean women organized this competition, which featured one event, a footrace of about 160 meters (175 yards) with separate heats for different age groups. According to Pausanias,

> Every four years the sixteen women weave a robe for Hera, and the same women hold Hera's games. The games are a running match between virgin girls; they run with their hair let down and their tunics rather above their knees, and the right breast and shoulder bared. The course for the race is the Olympic track, less about a sixth. They give the winners crowns made of olive-branches and a share of the ox they slaughter to Hera.[25]

Despite this off-season concession to female athletes, the main festival at Olympia, perhaps because of its rigidly conservative religious traditions, held out and continued to refuse women admittance. A famous story tells what happened when a mother who wanted to watch her son compete in the Olympic boxing matches in 404 B.C. sneaked in disguised as a trainer. The ruse worked until the young man won. Unable to contain her excitement, the mother leaped over the barrier separating the trainers from the boxers, in the process revealing her gender. In deference to her son, father, and brothers, all of whom were Olympic winners, the judges allowed her to go unpunished. But they instituted a new rule stipulating that henceforth trainers, like athletes, had to attend the contests in the nude.

Competing in the Nude

Exactly when Greek athletes began competing naked and why the custom developed remain unclear. Nearly all the scenes of sports contests depicted in ancient Greek sculpture and vase paintings show men competing in the nude. Yet many people today find it difficult to believe that the athletes, especially runners and wrestlers, did not wear loincloths (like modern jockstraps) to protect themselves. One recent explanation is that they *did* wear such protection and that artists left it out of their depictions as a matter of style, the better to accentuate the beauty of the nude body. In fact, Homer mentions wrestlers and boxers wearing loincloths in both the *Iliad* and the *Odyssey*. However, the fifth-century Athenian historian Thucydides claims that athletes originally wore protection but later discarded it:

> Formerly, even in the Olympic Games, the athletes who contended wore belts across their middles; and it is but a few years since that practice ceased. To this day among some of the barbarians [non-Greeks], especially in Asia . . . belts are worn by the combatants.[26]

Most available evidence supports the scenario that the use of loincloths gave way to nudity by at least the early fifth century B.C.

A number of theories have been proposed for why the athletes discarded clothes and protection. In one often-repeated story, a runner in the 720 B.C. Olympics, Orsippos of Megara, lost his

This modern depiction of various ancient Greek athletic games (including wrestling, boxing, running, and chariot racing) accurately shows most contestants performing in the nude.

loincloth in the middle of a race but was still able to win, thereby setting a trend. "A more likely reason," suggests Judith Swaddling, a classical scholar at the British Museum, "is that Greek men were always proud of their muscular, sun-tanned bodies, and were only too eager to contrast their excellent physical condition with that of barbarians who preferred to keep themselves covered up."[27] In this view, nudity in athletics was a way of showing Greek individuality, since the Greeks viewed physical shame as a form of barbarism. "In social terms," Vera Olivova adds,

> nudity was felt to distinguish the Greeks not only from the barbarians but from their own slaves, who were not allowed to share in physical training. Nudity was furthermore a link that bound all Greek citizens together. Just as the Athenian democratic system gradually overcame distinctions based on birth and wealth, so the discarding of clothes meant a nakedness that was common to all.[28]

Glory in Victory, Shame in Defeat

In modern times the supposed amateur status of ancient Greek athletes has proved even more controversial than their competing nude. Until the 1970s, the most widely accepted contention was that for a long time Greek athletes were amateurs who received no monetary awards and competed mainly for the love of sport. In this scenario, professionalism later crept in and corrupted the games' "pure" amateur spirit, an idea that led the early organizers of the modern Olympics to ban professional athletes. The supposed proof was that at the four ancient circuit festivals—at Olympia, Delphi, Isthmia, and Nemea—the victors received only crowns of leaves (which at Olympia were taken from a sacred olive tree in a grove near Zeus's temple).

In reality this theory is a myth; the modern concept of amateurism did not exist in ancient Greece. Although crowns of vegetation were indeed the sole prizes awarded at the circuit games, many athletes were subsidized by well-to-do patrons; and winning athletes always received numerous financial and other awards when they returned to their home cities. These often included valuable bronze tripods, ornamental cups, and jars of olive oil, which the athletes could sell for a profit, as well as cash awards. Moreover, all of the other hundreds of local festivals that featured games gave such prizes outright.

These awards were substantial. In late fifth-century B.C. Athens, a winning runner at the Panathenaea received one hundred jars of olive oil. Classical scholar David Young reckons that such jars were worth at least twelve drachmas each at the time, which makes the whole prize worth twelve hundred drachmas. Consider that the average Greek worker earned about one drachma per day (about three hundred drachma per year) in the late fifth century; this means that an athlete could receive the equivalent of four years' salary by winning a single footrace!

And often that was only the beginning. Like many other communities, Athens awarded native sons who had been victorious in the circuit games free meals for life. According to a surviving inscription, "All those who have won the athletic event at the Olympic, Pythian, Isthmian, or Nemean games shall have the right to eat free of charge in the city hall and also have other honors in addition to the free meals." [29] What is more, the most successful athletes were glorified almost as gods, as poets like Pindar composed odes and sculptors like Myron molded statues in their honor.

Such valuable prizes and honors were surely the principal inducement for men to train and compete in the games, especially the most prestigious ones. The idea of competing mainly out of simple love of sport and the desire to share good fellowship with other athletes, win or lose, is strictly a modern concept. To ancient Greek athletes, winning was imperative and defeat shameful. Typical is the epitaph of a boxer who died while competing: "Here [in Olympia] he died, boxing in the stadium, having prayed to Zeus for either the wreath or death, aged 35. Farewell." [30] And Epictetus writes, "In the Olympic Games you cannot just be beaten and then depart, but first of all, you will be disgraced . . . before the whole world." [31] Perhaps most powerful of all is Pindar's description of four losers at Delphi, "to whom the Pythian feast has given no glad homecoming. . . . They, when they meet their mothers, have no sweet laughter to cheer them up. . . . In back streets they cower, avoiding their enemies; disaster has bitten them."[32]

Did the Ancient Greeks Need Athletic Supporters?

Here, from his widely consulted sourcebook Sport and Recreation in Ancient Greece, *scholar Waldo Sweet suggests how ancient Greek athletes, who competed in the nude, may have avoided injuries to their genitals.*

"Neither visual nor literary references give us any reason to believe that Greek athletes in classical times wore any kind of athletic supporter. . . . How much protection do modern athletes need? A short questionnaire was distributed to members of the athletics staff and the Department of Classical Studies of the University of Michigan, asking among other things what events in the ancient Olympics would necessitate wearing equipment like a jockstrap. Of forty respondents, only six thought no protection would be needed. We have also talked with about a dozen nudists. While conceding the need for protection in a sport like football, they do not believe that most other sports require such support. One dedicated nudist reported. . . that he and his friends found that 'during vigorous physical activity the scrotum and penis retract into a tight, compact bundle, close to the body and removed from danger of injury.'. . . The muscle that lifts or drops the testicles is called the cremaster muscle. . . . Sumo wrestlers in Japan strengthen this muscle by exercise, often beginning in childhood. . . . Personal experience in running nude proved to this writer that absolutely no discomfort occurred and the genitals did in fact retract. It is quite likely that many or even most Greeks did without any protection for the genitals. Modern opinion on how much protection the ancient Greeks would need may not be valid. For example, most modern runners would need the protection of shoes in running long distances, but in August 1960 in Rome, the Olympic marathon was won by the barefoot Abebe Pikila from Ethiopia."

A Great Social and Religious Experience

Thus, unlike modern athletes who often compete against the clock or measuring tape in an effort to set records, Greek athletes cared little how far they threw or how fast they ran; beating the competition and winning first place was almost always the single-minded goal. This desire to win at nearly any cost sometimes led to cheating and bribery. In one celebrated case in 388 B.C., a boxer named Eupolius, from Thessaly in central Greece, bribed three rivals to let him win first place at Olympia. About half a century later an Athenian supposedly won the Olympic pentathlon the same way. No evidence exists, however, to suggest that such corruption was common at Olympia (although it may have been

An Olympic victor receives his crown of laurel leaves in a solemn ceremony not unlike those held for winners in the modern Olympics. Ancient Olympic winners enjoyed other fruits of victory, including valuable containers of olive oil.

The Buying Power of Victors' Prizes

In this portion of his well-known study of amateurism versus professionalism in ancient sports, The Olympic Myth of Greek Amateur Athletics, *historian David Young demonstrates the substantial worth of the prize received by the winner of an Athenian footrace.*

"An inscription from the first half of the fourth century [B.C.] records the amount of olive oil awarded as a prize to the victor in each category. The oil is priceable. We can easily arrive at an approximate value for the prizes in these games. . . . Because the prize for the men's *stade* was an even hundred amphoras [jars] of oil, it is most convenient to base the study on that. . . event, a footrace roughly equivalent to our 200-meter dash. The cheapest recorded price for olive oil in classical antiquity is twelve drachmas an amphora. . . . Thus, twelve drachmas per amphora is the *lowest* usable figure, and we must estimate the value of the stade victor's prize at a *minimum* of 1,200 drachmas. . . . The standard wage formula (one drachma = one day's wage) refers to the end of the fifth century and the start of the fourth (about 400 B.C.). . . . There is no need to inquire further to answer the main question. A single athletic victory . . . paid noticeably more money than a full year's work [in this case four full years' work]. . . . With his 1,200 drachmas, the victorious sprinter had a small fortune in purchasing power. For example, he could buy six or seven *medium*-priced slaves. . . or a flock of about 100 sheep. Or he could purchase outright two or three houses in Athens."

more widespread in less prestigious games; conclusive evidence is lacking).

Despite the possibility of widespread corruption in Greek athletics, most of the competitors, as is true today, were probably honest and fair. And the vast majority of both contestants and spectators enjoyed and benefited from attending the festival games. As University of Louisville scholar Robert Kebric aptly puts it,

Professionalism, politicism, bribery, racism, public adulation, as well as outrage and derision, were as much a part of ancient athletic contests as they are today—perhaps more so. Nonetheless, the games provided the Greeks with a great social and religious experience, and in the final analysis, the positive aspects of the competition probably outweighed the negative.[33]

2 The Glories of Physical Achievement: Running, Jumping, and Throwing

As Homer's *Iliad* and *Odyssey* show, the Greeks participated in diverse forms of sporting events, including running, wrestling, boxing, and chariot racing, well before the advent of the first games at Olympia. However, the Olympics, the first formal international contests held on a permanent basis, long featured just a few simple events involving three of the most basic physical actions—running, throwing, and jumping. The first thirteen Olympiads had only a single event, the *stade*, a footrace of about 183 meters (600 feet). Even after the addition of many others, this remained the games' most prestigious event, so much so that its winner received the honor of having the current Olympiad named after him. In 724 B.C. a second footrace, the *diaulos*, twice as long as the *stade*, was added; and the next Olympiad, in 720, introduced the *dolichos*, equivalent to twenty-four *stades* (somewhat less than 5 kilometers or 3 miles). These races, constituting in a sense the "triple crown" of running events, soon became the basic, staple features of Greek athletic games everywhere. The occasional runner who was able to win all three races in a single Olympiad received the coveted title of *triastes*, or "tripler." One sprinter, Leonidas of Rhodes, became legendary when he won all three running events at each of

four successive Olympiads (between 164 and 152 B.C.), surely one of history's most extraordinary athletic records.

A Line in the Dirt

During the first several Olympiads, there was still no formal stadium for these events. Instead, the judges drew a line in the dirt to mark the start, and the runners dashed to the finish line, which was located, rather appropriately considering the games' religious tenure, at Zeus's great altar.[34] Spectators watched from the slopes of the nearby hill of Kronos. Over time this simple rectangular running area underwent modest improvements, such as the addition of shallow banks of earth along the sides to accommodate more spectators. Finally, sometime around 350 B.C. the Greeks built a more permanent stadium, lined with stone blocks, several meters (yards) east of the original running area. Like the original, as well as tracks at other Greek sanctuaries, it was one *stade*, or *stadion*, long (*stadium* is the Latin, and therefore Roman, version of *stadion*). A *stade* was always about 183 meters (600 feet);[35] however, values for Greek measurement differed somewhat from place to place; so

Four Great Ancient Runners

In this excerpt from his famous ancient travelogue, the Guide to Greece *(Peter Levi's translation), Pausanias, who visited Olympia and other sites where games were held, provides information about four renowned runners.*

"Astylos of Kroton . . . won the running [i.e., the *stade*] three times in succession and scored victories in the two-lap race [the *diaulos*] as well. Because in his two last victories he proclaimed himself as a Syracusan [resident of the Greek city of Syracuse, in Sicily, which had more than once attacked Kroton] . . . the people of Kroton decreed that his house be turned into a prison and they destroyed his portrait in the sanctuary of Hera. . . . There is a Lykian called Hermogenes, who . . . carried off the wild olive [i.e., won the prize] eight times in three Olympics, and the Greeks nicknamed him "the Horse." Polites is another man you might well be really staggered by. Polites came from Keramos in Karia [in western Asia Minor], and at Olympia he proved himself a master of running of every kind. He could switch within the shortest period of time from the longest run to the shortest sprint. On the same day he won the long distance [*dolichos*] and the ordinary running [*stade*] and the two-laps [*diaulos*] as well. . . . The most distinguished of all running records belongs to Leonidas of Rhodes. He held out at the height of his speed for four Olympic cycles, and won twelve times."

while the stadium at Olympia measured 192.28 meters (about 631 feet), stadiums in other cities varied between 177 and 210 meters (581 and 689 feet).

Events involving the other two basic physical activities, throwing and jumping, entered the Olympic program in 708 B.C. with the addition of the pentathlon. This combination of five events was designed as a supreme test of the all-around athlete. It included the *stade*, which, of course, also continued to be held separately. The pentathlon also featured (in addition to wresting) the long jump and the discus and javelin throws, which were *not* held separately as they are today.[36] As might be expected, athletes who underwent the extensive training required to excel at running, jumping, and throwing tended to develop magnificent physiques. According to the famous fourth-century B.C. scholar Aristotle, "The pentathletes have the most beautiful bodies, because they are constructed for strength and speed together."[37] As models for Greek sculptors like Myron, whose discus thrower is world famous, these versatile athletes became eternal symbols of the glories of ancient Greek physical achievement.

The remains of the running area at Olympia, bordered by shallow banks of earth on which spectators stood or sat.

Starting Gates and Turning Posts

In some ways ancient runners and their events resembled their modern counterparts. Because so many contestants entered the games, there were, as there are today, several preliminary heats for each event. The runners drew lots from a bronze bowl to determine who would run in each heat; and the winners of the heats faced one another in the final showdown. As modern runners do, Greek runners approached the starting line and did some last-minute warm-up exercises. According to a contemporary witness, these included running in place, deep knee-bends, and practice starts. When everyone was ready, the signal for the start was either a trumpet blast or a judge's shout of "*Apite!*" ("Go!").

These similarities aside, ancient Greek footraces substantially differed from modern ones in two ways. The first involved the starting position the runners assumed. Instead of crouching down with one leg drawn back behind the body, like today's sprinters do, Greek runners stood upright with their arms stretched forward and their toes gripping a marble slab resting on the starting line. False starts sometimes occurred, just as they do today. The difference is that the ancient judges punished false-starters by having them publicly flogged. The problem was alleviated in large degree by the addition (in the fifth century B.C.) of a starting gate called a *hus-*

The marble starting slabs for the runners at Olympia, clearly showing the grooves in which they placed their toes.

Spectators cheer on the runners in the hoplitodromos, *or race in armor. The longest and most famous version of this event was held at Plataea, north of Athens.*

plex, which consisted of a series of horizontal bars in front of the runners. When the starter released a cord holding the bars, they all fell away at the same time, unleashing the runners. The second-century A.D. Greek writer Lucian describes the *husplex* while commenting on the runners' varying abilities and strategies:

> Once the *husplex* goes down, the good runner puts his mind only on going forward, and concentrating on the finish, puts his hope of victory in his legs. He does not foul the man next to him nor does he waste time thinking up tricks against his opponents. The immoral, unskilled athlete, however, turns his hope of success from speed to unsportsmanlike conduct, and the only thing in the world he thinks of is how to hold his opponent or check him by tripping, feeling that if he should fail to do this, he could never win.[38]

The second difference between ancient and modern footraces was the presence of a turning post, the *kampter*, at the opposite end of the stadium from the starting line. (Scholars are still unsure whether there was one post for all runners or one post for each runner.[39]) In races longer than the *stade*, the runners had to make hairpin turns and then run the opposite way, a maneuver modern athletes would find difficult and annoying.

The Race in Armor

The *stade*, *diaulos*, and *dolichos* were not the only footraces in the ancient Greek games. Another important event, introduced at Olympia in 520 B.C., was the race in armor, the *hoplitodromos*, which took its name from "hoplite," the term describing a heavily armored infantry soldier. The runners wore a

The Problem of Scoring the Pentathlon

One of the biggest unknowns about ancient Greek athletics is how the pentathlon, made up of five events, was scored. Several theories have been suggested, including a very complicated one by the late and noted scholar E. Norman Gardiner (see his Athletics of the Ancient World, *pp. 178–80). This more recent suggestion is by Waldo Sweet in* Sport and Recreation in Ancient Greece: A Sourcebook with Translations.

"All competitors competed in the first three events. If the same athlete won all three events, he was the outright winner, and events four and five were cancelled. If there was no winner at the end of event number three, all contestants competed in event number four, at the end of which there could have been only four combinations: 1. One athlete had won three of the four events; he was the winner, and the fifth event (wrestling) was cancelled. 2. Two athletes had each won two victories; they proceeded to the wrestling, where one of the two would win his third victory. 3. One athlete had scored two victories, and two other athletes had scored one apiece. 4. There had been a different victor in each of the four events. When there had been a different winner in each event . . . the four athletes . . . were matched by lot. Each pair then competed in an event selected by lot from an event *that neither athlete had won* in this competition. . . . The victors in these pairs would then have two victories each, and they would proceed to the wrestling, which would decide the winner. If there was one athlete with two victories and two with one win . . . the two with one victory would compete against each other in an event that neither had won; the winner of this match, who now had two victories, met in the wrestling with the other athlete with two victories, to determine the winner."

A muscular competitor throws his opponent in this handsome sculpture of Greek wrestlers.

bronze helmet and greaves (lower-leg protectors) and carried a bronze shield, or *hoplon*. Some evidence suggests that over time the helmet and greaves were eliminated, leaving only the burden of the shield.

The distance of this unusual race differed from place to place. At Olympia and Athens it seems to have been two *stades* (therefore equivalent to the *diaulos*), or about 385 meters (1,262 feet); at Nemea, it was four *stades* (less than a kilometer or about half a mile); and at Plataea, a small polis north of Athens, it was fifteen *stades* (3.2 kilometers or almost 2 miles). The Plataean hoplite race became the most famous in the ancient world, even more important than the one at Olympia. This was because Plataea was the site of a huge battle fought in 479 B.C., in which a united Greek army crushed an invading Persian force, saving Greece and perhaps all of Europe from Asian domination. As the second/third-century A.D. Greek writer Philostratus writes,

> The hoplite race at Plataea in Boeotia had the most prestige because of the length of the run and because of the long armor which reached to the feet and protected the athlete as if he were in battle [the author appears to refer here specifically to a shield larger than the customary *hoplon*]. It was also instituted to celebrate their accomplishments against the Persians; the Greeks had thought this [event] up to show contempt for the barbarians.[40]

The race in armor must have been viewed both seriously and humorously, depending on the time and place. On the serious side, appearing last on the program at Olympia and most other places, it was a reminder that all Greek athletic training had developed as a way of keeping citizen-soldiers fit for war. On the other hand, images of armored men clanking along, sometimes bumping into and falling over one another, and other times dropping their shields and scrambling to pick them up, often provoked laughter. In his comedy *Birds*, for instance, the fifth-century B.C. Athenian playwright Aristophanes poked fun at a group of characters dressed in feathered outfits by likening them to the armored runners in the *hoplitodromos*.

Other Footraces

Some ancient footraces were featured at various local festivals but not at Olympia and the other circuit games. One, the *hippios*, or "horsey race," did not actually involve horses. It was a human running event that was probably so named because its length, four *stades* (roughly 800 meters or half a mile), was the same as the length of the typical hippodrome, or horse-racing track. Torch races were also common in many local games. One, the *lampadedromia*, was a relay race in which the six-to-ten runners on each team passed a lit torch instead of a baton. In a passage from his guidebook, Pausanias describes what appears to be a nonteam torch race held in Athens. The contestants, he says, ran into the city from an altar dedicated to Prometheus, the legendary god who gave fire to humans. "The contest consists of running while keeping the torch alight; if the first man's torch is out he loses and the second man wins; if his is not burning either, the third man wins; if all the torches are out no one wins."[41] If there was indeed a winner, he was honored by having his

Torch races were common in Greek athletic games, although they were not featured at the Olympic and other circuit games. This ancient vase painting shows a torch runner outdistancing his opponent.

torch light the festival's sacrificial altar. The organizers of the modern Olympic Games borrowed this idea by having a lone runner carry a torch around the stadium and light the symbolic Olympic flame. But no such ceremony, nor any other event involving torches, took place at the ancient Olympics.

Contrary to popular belief, the marathon race (a long-distance run of 42 kilometers, 352 meters, or 26 miles, 385 yards), a widely popular sporting event today, did not exist in ancient times. Modern Olympic officials introduced it in 1896 to commemorate the legendary feat of Phidippides, an Athenian soldier and runner. Supposedly, following the 490 B.C. Battle of Marathon, in which the Athenian army defeated a much larger force of Persian invaders, Phidippides ran the 25 miles or so to Athens, proclaimed the victory, and dropped dead from exhaustion. It remains unclear whether this inspiring feat actually happened; but there is no doubt whatsoever that no Greek or Roman games ever featured a footrace nearly as long as the marathon.

Jumps Too Long to Be Believed?

Unlike running, which spawned many diverse ancient events, jumping produced only one—the long jump. The technique employed in this event was extremely different from that used by modern jumpers, principally because the ancients used handheld jumping weights called *halteres*. Philostratus comments on their use:

> The *halteres* . . . were invented for jumping, from which they take their name [since the Greek word for jumping was *halma*]. Considering the jump to be one of the most difficult events in competition, the rules permit encouragement of the jumper by means of a flute and also assist him even more with the *halteres*. For then guidance of the hands is unfailing and brings the feet to the ground without wavering and in good form [i.e., the feet must make a clean impression, or mark, in the sand]. The rules show how impor-

tant this is, for they [the judges] refuse to have the jump measured if the mark is not correct. Large sizes of *halteres* are used to exercise the arms and shoulders. . . . They should be used by the athletes [to train for] the light as well as heavy events in all exercises except those designed to relax the athlete.[42]

Exactly how flute-playing may have helped the jumpers is unknown. However, this important tract informs us that *halteres* not only helped ensure long, well-coordinated jumps but also doubled as dumbbells for strengthening the upper body. They consisted of lumps of lead or stone molded or carved with recessed areas for gripping

The jumper shown in this vase painting grips a pair of halteres, *jumping weights which were usually made of metal or stone.*

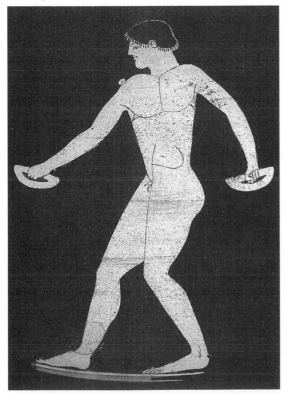

with the hands and varied in weight from about two to ten pounds each.

Modern jumpers attempting to re-create ancient long jumps have more or less confirmed the depictions of the event shown in ancient paintings. Upon his take-off, a jumper, holding a *haltere* in each hand, apparently swung them forward as forcefully as he could, giving him considerable forward momentum. As he came in for his landing, he swung the weights backward, providing a small amount of extra thrust, and then discarded them. The exact way all these movements were accomplished is somewhat uncertain, partly because modern athletes find the weights strange and awkward and therefore cannot be certain they are using them correctly. That ancient jumpers found their use perfectly natural is not surprising, considering that, as Robert B. Kebric points out, they probably originated as a military exercise. "The practice may have begun," he writes,

as a training technique to help soldiers become accustomed to managing their hand-held equipment effectively while jumping on the run during combat. Perfecting this technique undoubtedly took much time, and the fact that an athlete's jump was counted only if he landed upright in the pit is further indication of the event's military background. A soldier who jumped over an obstacle only to fall backward on the ground would have little chance of survival on the battlefield. Eventually, the exercise itself must have become a form of competition, and the training weights remained an integral part of it. The reason that modern athletes have had so much trouble recreating the ancient technique of long jumping is most likely because using weights is contrary to all that they have learned. For the ancient jumper, however, the event did not exist without the weights, and years of practice resulted in the complete coordination of the latter with body movement.[43]

The problem for modern historians is not the use of the weights but the fact that the jumps mentioned by ancient writers are much too long to be believed. Phayllus of Kroton, a military hero and renowned athlete, is said to have jumped about seventeen meters (fifty-five feet), for example.[44] And a jump of approximately sixteen

This statue of a discus thrower, now on display at the Louvre in Paris, captures the athlete in his moment of concentration just prior to a throw.

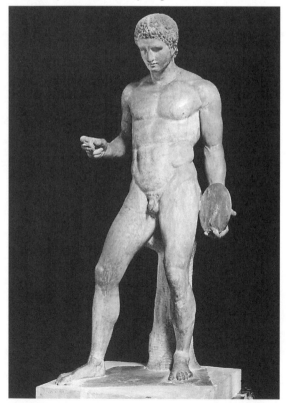

meters (fifty-two feet) is recorded for Chionis of Sparta. Even with *halteres* providing an extra boost, it seems physically impossible for these jumpers to have exceeded by over six meters (twenty feet) the present world record of approximately nine meters (just under thirty feet).

Various explanations have been posed for this discrepancy. The ancient texts may be in error; the Greeks may have been physically superior to modern people; the *halteres* were perhaps more efficient than shown in modern experiments; the "feet" used to measure ancient jumps may have been much shorter than the modern foot; or the ancient jump may actually have been a multiple jump, similar to the modern triple jump (or "hop, skip, and jump"). A majority of scholars presently favor the last of these—a multiple jump. This is supported by the fact that the modern record for the triple jump (about eighteen meters or fifty-eight feet) is in the same range as ancient records for the long jump. No solid ancient evidence has yet been found to support the theory, however; so for the time being the ancient long jump remains a bit of a mystery.

The Throwing Events

Some mystery also surrounds another event performed in the ancient pentathlon, namely the discus throw. This event seems to have originated as a custom in which contestants threw a valuable lump of metal and the winner got to keep the lump as his prize. For example, during Patroclus's funeral games in the *Iliad*, Achilles offers as a prize an ingot of iron, then considered quite valuable:

They [the throwers] stood in a row, and Epeios took up the weight, circled it round his head and threw it, and the people roared with laughter. Next to throw the weight was Leonteus. . . . Third, Telamonian Ajax lifted it and hurled it. The cast from the strong man went beyond the others. But when Polypoites raised the lump, he threw it as far beyond all the others as a herdsman sends his cudgel flying over the herds of cattle. There was a loud cheer, and his companions got up and carried away the prize to their camp.[45]

Over time, as such contests became part of regular Greek athletic programs, the objects thrown ceased to be the prizes and became merely pieces of equipment. Made of bronze or marble, they varied in weight but averaged about two and a half kilograms (about five and a half pounds), slightly more than a modern discus. At Olympia, the "official" discuses used in the games were stored in one of the treasuries north of Zeus's great altar. As was probably also customary at other athletic sites, having everyone in a competition throw the same discus ensured fairness.

The question that modern scholars are still unable to answer is exactly how ancient athletes threw the discus. Today, throwers complete a complex spin of almost two revolutions to build up centrifugal force and thereby attain a longer throw. Some scholars, among them the noted ancient sports expert H. A. Harris, believe that ancient throwers used a similar kind of spin; however, others contend that they made no more than a three-quarter turn before releasing the discus.[46] Unfortunately, ancient artistic depictions of discus-throwing, such as Myron's statue, are no help because they

An ancient warrior, perhaps in the Bronze Age, goes to hurl a javelin at an attacker. The Greek hoplites who developed in later times used their spears for jabbing rather than throwing.

tend to capture the athlete during his warm-up swing, not during the actual throw.

By contrast, the method for the other ancient throwing event, the javelin throw, is fairly well understood. Of all ancient sports, this was perhaps the most closely connected with warfare. At least as early as the Bronze Age, Mediterranean warriors used javelins, which they threw at enemies from a distance (as opposed to spears, which were heavier and used for thrusting during hand-to-hand fighting). Some ancient festivals included an event in which athletes mounted on horses tossed javelins at a target. But at Olympia the throwers competed strictly on foot, as they do in modern athletics.

In some ways the throwing technique used by ancient javelin throwers was identical to that employed by their modern counterparts. They ran up to the throwing line carrying the javelin in the right hand,

An Eyewitness to Ancient Olympia

Here, from his Guide to Greece, *Pausanias describes parts of the Olympic stadium and training ground (gymnasium) as they appeared in the second century* A.D.

"At the end of the [row of] statues [of Zeus] erected from athletes' penalties is what they call the Hidden Entrance [to the stadium], through which the Greek judges and the competitors enter the stadium. The stadium is a mound of earth, but it has a [stone] seat built for the officials. Opposite the Greek judges is a white stone altar and on this altar a woman sits and watches the Olympic games, the priestess of Demeter of the Ground, an office awarded by Elis to different women at different times. . . . By the end of the stadium where they have made the starting-place for the sprinters is the grave of Endymion [an early king of Elis], so the Eleans say. . . . Training for the pentathlon and for running takes place in the training-ground at Olympia; there is a stone platform there in the open air where originally a trophy [prize] for a victory over Arkadia used to stand. There is another smaller enclosure on the left of the entrance to the training-ground, where the competitors have their wrestling pits. The athletes' houses face southwest by the wall of the east colonnade of the training-ground."

keeping the javelin in a more or less horizontal position, and extended the left arm during the throw to maintain proper balance. The major difference between ancient and modern technique was the ancients' use of a leather thong, or strap, called the *ankyle.* Keeping the javelin's shaft cradled in his palm, the thrower inserted two or three fingers into a loop in the thong, the rest of which wound around the middle of the shaft. As he let the javelin fly, the thong rapidly unwound, giving the javelin a spin that ensured a steadier flight, although not necessarily greater distance.[47]

The distances for ancient javelin throws are unknown and most may never even have been recorded. As in other athletic events, winning, rather than setting records, was the all-important goal. "The best Greek athletes," Harris summarizes, "were content to defeat those who were in immediate competition with them, and did not care what others had done at other times and places."[48]

Chapter

3

Muscle Mass and Raw Courage: The Grueling Athletic Combat Events

Among the most popular of ancient sports were those involving combat between two competitors. These events can be divided into two general groups—those featuring weapons, which included Rome's gladiatorial fights, and those without weapons. The latter included wrestling, boxing, and the *pankration*, or "all-in fighting," a rough and tumble combination of wrestling, boxing, and street fighting. These three events were regular and popular features of Greek athletic games, so, for convenience, they are here termed *athletic combat events* to differentiate them from the more lethal variety practiced in Rome. For the most part, the Romans did not care much for wrestling or the *pankration*, although they did enjoy boxing. Perhaps this was because they were particularly fond of the most dangerous and bloody entertainments, and boxing was viewed as the most brutal of the three weaponless combat events. The injuries suffered by a boxer named Olympikos, who, according to one ancient source, "used to have nose, chin, forehead, ears, and eyelids," were not unusual. Supposedly he lost an important lawsuit because he no longer bore any resemblance to an earlier portrait and was therefore "judged to be an imposter."[49]

Boxers adorn a sculpted relief found at Rome. Both the Greeks and Romans enjoyed watching boxing, considered the most violent and dangerous of ancient weaponless games. Serious injuries were common and some boxers died.

There is no mystery about the origins of these popular athletic combat events. Their very name indicates that they were intimately related to training for and participation in warfare. According to Philostratus,

> Wrestling and the *pankration* were introduced [into athletic competitions] because of their application to war. The usefulness of the first event was made clear by the action at [the Battle of] Marathon, where the Athenians fought in such a way as to seem to be almost wrestling. The usefulness of the second was shown at [the Battle of] Thermopylae, where the Spartans [who were bravely holding back a vastly larger force of Persians], after their swords and spears were broken, fought effectively with their bare hands.[50]

This ancient connection between war and athletic competition cannot be overstated. As Michael Poliakoff, an authority on ancient combat sports, states,

Warfare was an inescapable reality of the ancient world, and it exercised profound influence on civic and political life. . . . Ancient states had to face the question of how to meet the regular, if not constant, sequence of military exigencies [emergencies] that threatened their existence. Some states like Sparta and early Rome chose to keep their citizens in perpetual readiness for war; others, like Athens, relied to a large degree on the conscientiousness of the citizenry to be physically and emotionally ready for immediate muster. . . . Certainly war gives a partial explanation for Greek society's toleration of violent athletics. It was at best an indirect means of training soldiers.[51]

Thus it was that most young Greek males, even if they never entered formal competitions, regularly engaged in informal bouts of wrestling, boxing, and *pankration*, much as young Americans grow up playing backyard football and basketball.

Two wrestlers grapple as their instructor (at left) looks on. Young Greeks wrestled informally, much as modern children play backyard ball games.

Combat Sports in Sparta

Sparta took a different, and more violent, approach to combat sports. Military training began when boys were about seven. At twenty, a youth joined one of two teams which regularly engaged in brutal games. Scholar Michael Poliakoff explains these in this excerpt from Combat Sports in the Ancient World.

"Each year the two youth teams would gather on an island, fighting each other wildly, gouging, biting, and punching, until one team drove the other into the water. Spartans also had team sports that involved quite a lot of fighting over the ball. . . . The most shocking of all Spartan 'utilitarian' contests was the yearly ritual at the festival of Artemis [goddess of hunting], in which Spartan boys would submit to flogging, vying to see who could stand the pain and loss of blood longest. . . . Image abroad also mattered. Although Sparta permitted a high level of violence in *pankration*, allowing the biting and gouging banned elsewhere in Greece, Sparta forbade her citizens to compete abroad in either *pankration* or boxing. The state could accept a Spartan losing abroad in a contest of skill, like running . . . but not in a fighting event."

Many modern youngsters learn to box and wrestle, too. Unlike today's boxing and wrestling, however, ancient combat sports did not have separate weight classes designed to allow athletes of all sizes to compete, so the largest and strongest contestants usually won. Because there were also no time limits, a high degree of toughness and endurance, which the Greeks called *kartereia*, was as essential as muscle mass. The following description by a first-century A.D. writer vividly demonstrates the special kind of qualities needed to win in these grueling events.

I already witnessed once in a *pankration* contest a man who hurled blows with hands and feet, all of them well-directed, leaving nothing undone that might bring him victory, but who gave up, was worn out, and finally left the stadium uncrowned. The man being battered, on the other hand, was compact with solid flesh, mean, tough, exuding the athlete's spirit, and all muscle, like a stone or iron—he didn't give in to the blows and broke the force of his opponent by the toughness and firmness of his endurance until he won the final victory.[52]

Wrestling

Though wrestling required this same degree of strength and endurance, it also demanded, perhaps more than boxing or *pankration*, a high degree of scientific skill, strategy, and cunning. For the ancient

One's Opponent Determined by Lot

This excerpt from Hermotimos, *by the second-century* A.D. *Greek satirist Lucian of Samosata (as translated in Waldo Sweet's* Sport and Recreation in Ancient Greece*), describes how the competitors in wrestling and other combat sports drew lots to determine the various pairings.*

"A silver vase sacred to the god is put out in front. Into it are thrown small lots, as large as a bean with letters on them. There are two marked with an alpha [the first letter in the Greek alphabet], two with a beta [the second letter], and so with the others. . . . Then each of the athletes comes up and, with a prayer to Zeus, puts his hand in the vase and pulls out one of the lots. After him another does the same thing. . . . [Then a judge or other official] looks at their lots and . . . matches in wrestling or pankration the man holding an alpha with the person holding the other alpha. Then in the same way he matches beta with beta. . . . He does it this way if the competitors are even in number . . . but if they are odd . . . he mixes in with the other matched lots an odd lot with a letter on it which does not match any other. Whoever draws this lot waits . . . while the other pairs fight. And this is a considerable advantage to an athlete, to be able to compete fresh against competitors who are fatigued."

Greeks, wrestling training constituted the most important part of physical education; and Greek society expected that an accomplished male adult would enjoy and participate in wrestling as much as he would reading or discussing politics with his friends. Wrestling was so important a part of Greek life that, by the fifth century B.C., almost every Greek town had a *palaestra*, a wrestling facility or a section of a gymnasium devoted to wrestling.[53]

There were two general types of Greek wrestling, "upright" and "ground." Both began with the fighters in a standing position. The difference was that in upright wrestling, which was the only version allowed in formal competitions, the main object was to throw one's opponent to the ground. This constituted a fall (as opposed to modern amateur wrestling, in which holding an opponent's shoulders to the mat gains a fall). Three falls were required for a victory. Therefore, a winning wrestler was referred to as a *triakter*, or "tripler." In ground wrestling, practiced mainly in the *palaestra*, after a successful throw the fighters continued to grapple on the ground until one acknowledged defeat (the signal for which was an upraised hand).

Many of the exact rules for and moves used in these events are uncertain. In general it seems that tripping was allowed and that leg holds were either prohibited or rarely used. Parts of a wrestling manual discovered on a papyrus roll and dated to the first or second century A.D. describe some apparently common holds and strategies:

> You throw him. You stand up and turn around. You fight it out. . . . You take a hold around him. You get under his hold. You step through and fight it out. You underhook with your right arm. You wrap your arm around his, where he has taken the underhook, and attack the side with your left foot. You push away with your left hand. You force the hold and fight it out.[54]

Punching and eye gouging were, of course, prohibited. And a late sixth-century decree, recently unearthed at Olympia, forbade wrestlers from breaking their opponents' fingers. The judges stood by holding large rods, ready to mete out painful blows to rule-breakers. Such punishments must have been fairly common, for ancient evidence indicates that, at least during competition matches, ancient wrestlers fought bitterly hard and often re-

sorted to brutal tactics. The use of dangerous strangleholds was not uncommon, for example. And despite the prohibition against breaking fingers, in the mid-fifth century B.C. a Sicilian Greek named Leontiskos twice won his Olympic wrestling matches using this very tactic. (Pausanias later saw his statue at Olympia, appropriately beside that of a *pankrationist* named Sostratos, whose frequent employment of the move earned him the nickname of "Mr. Fingertips."[55])

The Incredible Milo

Leontiskos's considerable reputation was tiny, however, in comparison to that of the most famous, and probably the greatest, wrestler in Western history—Milo of Kroton. This remarkable athlete, who, it was said, no one ever managed to bring to his knees, collected his first crown when he won the boys' wrestling match at Olympia

A vase painting shows two wrestlers competing while a judge stands holding a rod. If the judge perceived an infraction, he immediately gave the rule-breaker a painful whack.

in 540 B.C. He then went on to win the men's wrestling matches at five successive Olympiads between 532 and 516; and he also won the wrestling competition at the Pythian Games six times, the Isthmian ten times, and the Nemean nine times.

Ancient sources say that Milo was a huge man. This makes sense since, as Poliakoff suggests, "only a huge and strong man could sufficiently compensate for waning endurance, and so continue to dominate the competitions for so many years."[56] Numerous legends grew up about him. Some may have been factual, or

This impressionistic depiction of the Great Milo of Kroton was created by the renowned French artist Paul Cézanne sometime between 1870 and 1890.

nearly so, while others, like those surrounding another famous Greek strongman, Heracles, border on the superhuman. Supposedly, for example, Milo carried a full-grown bull on his shoulders around the entire Olympic sanctuary and then butchered and devoured it that same day. Pausanias records some of his other legendary feats:

> He could hold a pomegranate so that no one could force him to release it, and yet the pressure of his hand did it no damage; and he could stand on an oiled discus and laugh at people flinging themselves at him and trying to shove him off. And there were other spectacular things he did. He tied a string around his brows like a ribbon or a wreath, and by holding his breath and filling the veins of his head with blood, he snapped the string with the power of his veins. He is supposed to have kept his right elbow by his side and held out his forearm straight to the front with the hand turned thumb uppermost and fingers flat: yet no one could shift his little finger.[57]

While Milo was competing at Olympia for the sixth time, his renowned undefeated streak finally ended. A much younger wrestler, Timotheos, also from Kroton, either tied or defeated him by avoiding close fighting and wearing out the bigger, older man. Yet Milo was so popular that a crowd of cheering fans, Timotheos among them, lifted Milo up and triumphantly carried him around the stadium. The great wrestler's death was tragic, however. Supposedly he was walking through the woods one day and spotted a partially felled tree with the wedges (used

Boxers Hammer Ribs and Rattle Teeth

This is the opening section of the vivid description of a boxing match that appears in the fifth book of the Aeneid, *Rome's national epic, penned by the first-century B.C. poet Virgil (translated here by Patric Dickinson).*

"The son of Anchises [Aeneas] held up two equal pairs of gloves, and as part of his office, bound them about the hands of both contestants. At once each took his guard, and without fear lifted his arms in the air, dancing on tip-toe. They held their heads up and well out of range and sparred for an opening, probing at each other—Dares quicker on foot, reliant on youth, Entellus the more powerful and the bigger, but slow and weak in the knee, and out of condition, panting for every breath, his huge limbs heaving. Many blows they aimed at each other and missed. Many blows hammered their hollow sides or thudded on ribs. Their fists kept lashing round forehead and ears, and uppercuts to the jaw rattled their teeth."

to split the trunk) still deeply implanted. He thought he could finish the job with his bare hands, but in the process the wedges fell out and the trunk trapped his hands. That night, defenseless for the first time in his life, he fell prey to a pack of wolves.

Boxing

The second of the three ancient athletic combat events, boxing, was widely viewed as the most dangerous and punishing. To be sure, boxing required a certain degree of skill and strategy, as it does today. But also like today, strength and endurance were a boxer's chief assets; and the object of the sport was to pound one's opponent into submission. Therefore, serious injuries, especially of the face and head, were common. Moreover, if an ancient boxer did not lose consciousness or give up, he ran a real risk of being beaten to death, as illustrated in this extremely vivid third-century B.C. description of a match:

All the [spectators] shouted in unison, when they saw the damage Amykos had suffered around his mouth and jaw. As his face swelled, his eyes started to close. Then Polydeuces . . . confused his opponent by feinting [pretending to move] from all directions. And when he saw that Amykos was confused, he smashed his fist into his opponent's brow, right over the nose, and opened up his forehead to the bone. And Amykos lay stretched out on his back among the flower petals. When he regained his feet, the battle became fierce. The blows they aimed at one another were meant to kill. . . . Polydeuces the unbeaten pounded his opponent's whole face into a shapeless mass with disfiguring blows. . . . On the ground lay Amykos, all of him, with his wits wandering, and he held up both hands in surrender, for he was near death.[58]

This sort of relentless pounding could go on because ancient boxing had no rounds—with short rest periods, swigs of water, and medical attention between—as modern boxing does. There were also no rings with ropes and corners for the boxers to back into. This tended, as the noted scholar E. Norman Gardiner suggests, "to discourage close fighting and to encourage defensive and waiting tactics."[59] Caution was of the utmost importance, for if one fighter fell down, his opponent was free to keep hitting him while he was down; needless to say, few in that perilous position were able to regain their footing.

Compounding the physical damage caused by such free-for-all tactics was that caused by the "gloves" worn by ancient boxers. Until about the middle of the fourth century B.C., Greek boxers wrapped light rawhide thongs around their wrists and hands. These thongs often did not cover the knuckles. In any case they were intended to keep the wearer from injuring his own hands rather than to reduce the chance of his seriously injuring his opponent, as is the case today. After the fourth century B.C. the Greeks began using what they called "hard" or "sharp" thongs, which were actual gloves with a heavy, hardened leather pad wrapped around the knuckles. These thongs provided the wearer with a cutting edge that could (and often did) easily slice open an opponent's flesh.

Roman boxing gloves caused even more damage and were often lethal. Such a glove, called a *caestus*, was similar to a Greek hard thong, except that it continued on up the arm almost to the shoulder; more importantly, the knuckle area of the Roman version was studded with metal lumps and spikes, sometimes as long as a person's finger. The great first-century B.C. Roman poet Virgil describes a *caestus* in his *Aeneid*. His assertion that "you can still see the bloodstains and the splayed fragments of brain"[60] on the device did not exaggerate the horrendous damage it routinely inflicted.

Winning—Their Only Pleasure?

Some evidence suggests that ancient boxers had even more to worry about than serious injuries and the high risk of dying while competing. More often than not, especially in the case of Roman boxers, their training began at a young age and consumed most of their time, denying them the chance for good educations or other normal pursuits. "These professional fighters," Vera Olivova comments,

> born in poverty or in primitive conditions of remote and backward areas . . . and excluded from any intellectual activity, were made still more savage by their training and by the contests themselves. They would travel with their trainers from one engagement to another, showing off their hard-won skill to pitiless, sensation-hungry spectators. Neither danger, nor injury could deflect them from their career . . . and they were, indeed, incapable of other work. Ancient writers testify that they were not even serviceable as soldiers, so one-sided was their training.[61]

One ancient writer, the first-century A.D. Greek orator Dio Chrysostom, suggested that winning prizes was the only pleasure that most boxers could look forward to in life. Here, he describes two men discussing a well-known boxer who had recently passed away:

> "With all these wonderful qualities, he came to an unhappy end, having endured the agony of athletics without experiencing the pleasures of life. And he was so eager to win that when he was dying he asked his friend . . . how many days of competition were left." And as he said this the old man began to cry. . . . Said I, "You should not say he came to an unhappy end. Quite the opposite. . . . You spoke about the pleasures he has missed. Whoever enjoyed more pleasure than an athlete eager to win who was always victorious and who knew that he was an object of admiration? In my opinion, the gods loved him very much, and they especially honored him by his death, so that he might experience none of the sorrows of life. For it is certain that if he had continued to live he would have become uglier rather than more beautiful, weaker instead of stronger, and in the same way might have suffered defeat. But any man who dies in the midst of the greatest honors after he has done mighty deeds has died the happiest of deaths." [62]

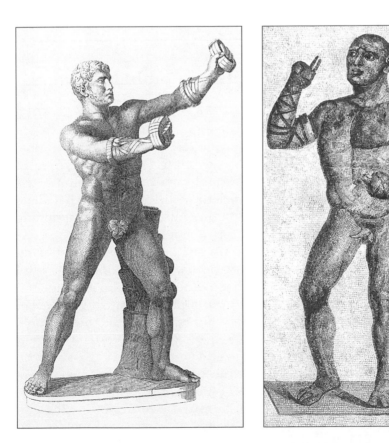

A Greek boxer (in the drawing of a statue at left) wears leather thongs, while a Roman boxer (in the mosaic at right) sports a deadly caestus *on each forearm.*

The *Pankration*

The *pankration* was not usually as dangerous or lethal as boxing, although evidently some *pankrationists* did die from time to time. A late classical writer named Philostratus (not the author of *On Athletics*) describes how a competitor named Arrichion died when his opponent applied a body scissors and a choke hold:

> Arrichion's opponent had him seized around the waist and was intending to kill him, and already he had thrust his forearm under Arrichion's throat to strangle him, having previously wrapped his legs around the groin . . . and he forestalled his [Arrichion's] resistance by strangling him until drowsy death came over Arrichion's senses.[63]

Despite unfortunate cases like that of Arrichion, injuries and deaths were so much more common in boxing that, as Pausanias reports, a competitor who had enrolled in both *pankration* and boxing at Olympia requested that *pankration* be held first (boxing normally came first). That way he "could fight before getting cut up in the boxing."[64]

The word *pankration* (*pancratium* in Latin) means "complete victory" in Greek and is probably derived from an older word meaning "total fight." In many ways it resembled modern professional wrestling (except that it was not staged entertainment in which the fighters know beforehand who is going to win). Punching, kicking, throwing, pressure locks, and strangling were all allowed; the only forbidden moves were biting and eye-gouging. A match ended only when one fighter surrendered, lost consciousness, or died.

The fact that biting and gouging were banned does not mean that no one employed them, of course. In the heat of battle, combatants, particularly those who feared they might lose, sometimes resorted to dirty tactics. Meanwhile, as they did in wrestling, the judges stood by with rods, ready to punish anyone who committed a foul. A fifth-century Greek *kylix* (drinking cup) now in the British Museum actually shows one *pankrationist* gouging another's eye while an official raises his rod to strike him. How often such offenders went on to win the *pankration* is unknown. But it is certain that some *pankrationists*, as well as wrestlers and boxers, were willing to endure a few whacks of the rod if some well-placed gouges or other dirty tactics gave them the clear advantage. Winning, after all, was everything.

Multiple Combat Winners

Even more important and prestigious than winning one of these athletic combat events was winning two or even three of them. Various surviving inscriptions and other ancient writings indicate that some fighters won one event, perhaps the wrestling match, at one festival and later won a different one, such as the boxing event, at another competition. A handful of gifted athletes managed to go a step farther and win multiple combat victories in the same competition or even on the same day. The most distinguished all-around fighter was Theogenes of Thassos, who lived in the early fifth century B.C. Theogenes, who won a staggering total of some thirteen hundred victories in boxing and *pankration* over the course of a long career,

A pankrationist *jumps on his opponent in a modern sketch recreating the combat event in which there were almost no rules or restrictions.*

was the first person to win both events in one day (at the Isthmian Games), a feat he later repeated. "Your mother, the island of Thassos, is blessed, Theogenes," reads a fourth-century B.C. inscription found at Delphi, "because of all the Greeks you have the greatest reputation for strength. . . . In nine Isthmian Games you won ten victories, for in the assembly the herald announced you alone of all mortals twice in the same day as victor, in the boxing and in the pankration."[65]

So far as is known, only one athlete won all three events—wrestling, boxing, and *pankration*—on the same day. He was Kleitomachos, who earned his triple crown in 216 B.C. at the Isthmian Games. Though he did not amass the huge number of victories and enjoy the fame that Theogenes did, his feat, requiring a unique mixture of muscle mass and raw courage, was nonetheless memorable. Few, if any, of today's athletes possess the physical and intestinal fortitude needed to face three fighters of the size and caliber of Mike Tyson or Hulk Hogan on the same day and beat them all. Indeed, today's complete absence of a sports competition offering the chance for someone to accomplish such a feat represents a major difference between classical and modern athletics.

4 Bloodshed and Killing as Spectacle Sports: The Roman Games

Except for boxing and chariot racing, most Romans had little interest in Greek athletics and much preferred their own spectacle sports, staged in large stone arenas called amphitheaters. These included fights between men and men, beasts and men, and beasts and beasts; wild animal hunts; and staged naval battles. All involved some measure of bloodshed and killing, whereas in Greek athletics serious injuries and death were rare and associated almost solely with boxing and the *pankration*. The most important difference between Greek and Roman sport, however,

This modern illustration shows armed arena hunters fighting wild animals, including a large bull, in the vast and crowded Roman Colosseum.

centered on the issue of citizen participation. The vast majority of Romans greatly enjoyed watching large-scale, violent games, which they viewed as a form of entertainment; but for a Roman citizen actually to participate in such public spectacles was viewed as improper, undignified, and socially unacceptable. This view was completely contrary to that of Greek society, which encouraged and glorified athletic participation by citizens.

One reason for this Roman disdain for Greek-style athletics was undoubtedly pride. The Romans were, for much of their history, a conservative, austere people who, like the Greek Spartans, took special pride in their military prowess and considered losing in battle the ultimate disgrace. Simply put, for most Romans defeat in an athletic competition was too much like defeat in war. As scholar David Young remarks, "No Roman could stand the risk of losing such an individual test, of looking inferior in public. To do it naked in full view of one's enemies would have made Roman blood run cold."[66] The famous first-century B.C. orator and senator Cicero expressed a typical Roman view of Greek games when he quoted with approval the words of an earlier Roman writer: "To strip in public is the beginning of evil-doing."[67]

Thus, status-conscious Romans, especially members of the upper classes, who presented themselves as models of public behavior, preferred to confine their competitive spirit to the battlefield, the political sphere, and the law courts. Indeed, Roman aristocrats consistently attempted to shape Roman attitudes toward watching as well as participating in sports. And Roman leaders, particularly the emperors, came to use sporting spectacles and other entertainments as means of appeasing and manipulating the urban masses.

Fears of Decadence

These uniquely Roman spectacles developed gradually during the same period in which the Romans conquered Greece and were first exposed to Greek athletics. During the late Republic (ca. 200–30 B.C.), most Roman aristocrats consistently rejected Greek-style games as effeminate (unmanly) and morally decadent. This attitude softened somewhat in the early Empire (ca. 30 B.C.–A.D. 180) as a few of the emperors instituted their own versions of Olympic competitions. The first emperor, Augustus, for example, founded the Actian Games to celebrate his victory over Antony and Cleopatra in the Battle of Actium in 31 B.C.; Nero, the egotistical fifth emperor, established the Neronian Games in Rome in the A.D. 60s; and around A.D. 132 the emperor Hadrian, an avid admirer of Greek culture, attempted to replace the games held at Olympia with a new festival in Athens (a move that failed when most Greek athletes, out of reverence for tradition, refused to attend).

During these years a fair number of lower-class Romans began attending such athletic games along with Greeks. Yet most leading Romans continued to promote the puritanical idea that such attendance was a symptom of society's moral decay. Commenting on Nero's games, the first/second century A.D. Roman historian Tacitus summarizes this view:

Traditional morals, already gradually deteriorating, have been utterly ruined

The first-century Roman emperor Nero, depicted here, sponsored Greek-style athletics, but they remained largely unpopular among the Romans.

century B.C., a number that continued to grow). Because most work was suspended on these holidays, large numbers of poor urban Romans were idle for long periods of time. Many senators and other leaders harbored the paranoid fear that the so-called mob, hungry and having too little to occupy its time, might protest, riot, or even rebel. Especially dangerous, in this view, was allowing large numbers of commoners to congregate in one place since it might lead to civil disturbances and the erosion of state authority; consequently, the Senate long refused to approve the construction of large, permanent theaters and amphitheaters.

Bread and Circuses

by this imported laxity! . . . Foreign influences demoralize our young men into shirkers, gymnasts, and perverts. Responsibility rests with emperor and Senate. They have given immorality a free hand [by approving and staging such games]. . . . It only remains to strip and fight in boxing-gloves instead of joining the army. . . . This vileness continues even at night! Good behavior has no time left for it. In these promiscuous crowds [of spectators], debauchees [sex maniacs and perverts] are emboldened to practice by night the lusts they have imagined by day.[68]

As late as the beginning of the first century B.C., leading Romans frowned on most Roman games as well, arguing that they promoted public laziness. In addition, the Romans observed many public holidays (at least fifty-seven by the mid–first

As public games became increasingly popular, these fears proved groundless. Roman leaders found that public spectacles, controlled by aristocrats and/or the state, could actually be potent tools for maintaining public order. So they made these games part of a two-fold policy. First, the government sponsored regular large-scale distributions of bread and other foodstuffs to the poor. By the late first century A.D., as many as 150,000 urban Romans received such handouts at hundreds of distribution centers located across the capital city. Senators, military generals, and emperors also spent huge sums subsidizing public festivals, shows, and games. This policy of appeasing the masses with free food and entertainment eventually became known as *panem et circenses*, or "bread and circuses," in reference to a famous sarcastic remark by the first-century A.D. humorist Juvenal. "There's only two things that concern" the commoners, he said, "bread and [circus] games."[69]

Although Juvenal referred specifically to chariot races (*ludi circenses*), he meant to include all public spectacles, shows, and games. Next to the races, the most popular of these were the *munera*—gladiatorial and wild animal fights staged in amphitheaters like Rome's famous Colosseum. The number of holidays on which *munera* were held each year is unclear. Such games were very expensive to produce and likely took place only on special occasions and therefore, on an irregular basis. Like Greek games, some were associated, at least at first, with traditional religious festivals, the *feriae*.[70] Thus the *Ludi Romani*, a large fifteen-day-long festival held each September to honor Jupiter (the Roman equivalent of Zeus), came to feature amphitheater games. The *munera*, along with other spectacles, also often celebrated the memory of important secular events, most notably military victories.

Along with a number of other customs and ideas, the Romans borrowed gladiatorial combats from an earlier Italian people, the Etruscans.[71] The Etruscans believed that when an important man died his spirit required a blood sacrifice to survive in the afterlife (hence, the literal translation of *munera*: "offerings" or "obligations" to the dead); so outside these individuals' tombs they staged rituals in which warriors fought to the death. In Rome the *munera* were at first private affairs staged by

The imposing remains of the Colosseum, inaugurated by the emperor Titus (reigned 79-81), Rome's most splendid and famous amphitheater.

aristocrats. Over time, however, both they and the general populace came to view these games more as entertainment than funeral ritual and demand grew for making gladiator bouts part of the public games. The renowned general Julius Caesar was the first leader to stage large-scale public *munera*. His first/second century A.D. Greek biographer Plutarch reported that in 65 B.C. Caesar presented 320 pairs of gladiators;[72] while according to Plutarch's contemporary, the Roman historian Suetonius,

> Caesar put on a gladiatorial show, but had collected so immense a troop of combatants that his terrified political

A nineteenth-century drawing of the great Roman general Julius Caesar, who organized spectacular gladiator fights during his steady rise to power in the 60s B.C.

opponents [fearing he might use these warriors against them] rushed a bill through the [legislature], limiting the number of gladiators that anyone might keep in Rome; consequently far fewer pairs fought than had been advertised.[73]

It was Caesar who provided a bridge from the older system of training and managing gladiators to the one that prevailed in the Empire. Before his time, a well-to-do individual who wanted to put on a gladiatorial show went to a professional supplier called a *lanista*, who procured and trained the fighters. Desiring to give the state more control over these fights, Caesar built a gladiator school run by senators and other prestigious Romans. Following his lead, his adopted son, Augustus, and the other early emperors soon made staging the *munera* virtually an imperial monopoly. State control and promotion of the games was a crucial factor in the rapid transformation of their bread-and-circuses policy into an ingrained institution.

The Various Kinds of Gladiators

The gladiators who fought in these games were mostly prisoners, slaves, and criminals who trained long and hard in schools like the one Caesar built; although a few such fighters were paid volunteers. Some of the latter became involved because they had financial difficulties, and these events offered generous prize money for the winners. Other volunteers were motivated by the physical challenge and appeal of danger or the prospect of becoming popular idols and sex symbols who could have their

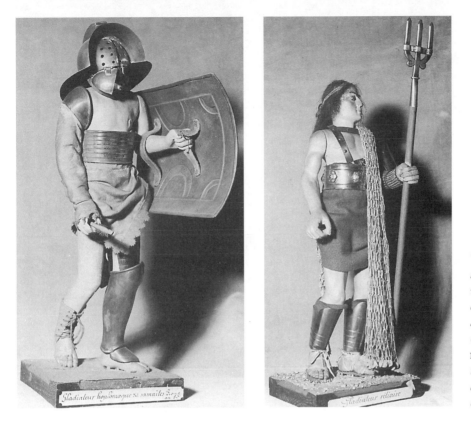

The models pictured here depict two of the most common kinds of gladiators—the Samnite, *or* secutor (*at left*), *and the* retiarius, *carrying the net he used to ensnare his opponents.*

pick of pretty young women. Among the graffiti slogans still scrawled on walls at Pompeii, the famous Roman town preserved under a layer of volcanic ash, are: "Caladus, the Thracian, makes all the girls sigh," and "Crescens, the net fighter, holds the hearts of all the girls."[74]

The terms "Thracian" and "net fighter" referred to the customary division of gladiators into various types and categories. Among the four main types that had evolved by the early Empire was the heavily armed Samnite, later called a *hoplomachus* or *secutor*. (The Romans may have recognized these three as separate and distinct types, but any such distinctions are now unclear; all employed basically the same weapons and tactics.) A Samnite carried a sword or a lance, a *scutum* (the rectangular

shield used by Roman legionary soldiers), a metal helmet, and protective armor on his right arm and left leg. Another type, the Thracian (so named because he resembled fighters from Thrace, a region of northern Greece), was not as elaborately armed. He wielded a curved short sword, the *sica*, and a small round shield, the *parma*. A third kind of gladiator, the *murmillo*, or "fishman" (after the fish-shaped crest on his helmet), was apparently similar to a Samnite but less heavily armed. A *murmillo* customarily fought still another kind of warrior, the *retiarius*, or "net-man," who wore no armor at all. A *retiarius* attempted to ensnare his opponent in his net (or used the net to trip the other man) and then to stab him with a long, razor-sharp trident, or three-pronged spear.

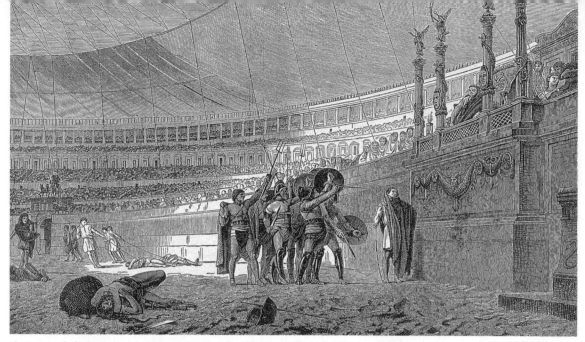

A group of gladiators salute the emperor after defeating their opponents, while attendants dressed as the god Mercury clear away the bodies.

In addition to the pairings of these main gladiator types, there were a number of special and off-beat types and pairings. These included *equites*, who fought on horseback using lances, swords, and/or lassoes; the *essedarii*, who confronted each other on chariots; and, perhaps the most bizarre of the lot, the *andabatae*, who grappled while blindfolded by massive helmets with no eyeholes. Women gladiators came into vogue under the emperors Nero and Domitian in the late first century A.D. Evidence shows that Domitian sometimes pitted female fighters against male dwarves as well as against one another.

"We Who Are About to Die Salute You!"

On the eagerly anticipated day when *munera* were scheduled at the Colosseum

or another amphitheater, the gladiators first entered the arena in a colorful parade known as the *pompa*. This was similar in some ways to the procession of the athletes on opening day of the modern Olympic Games. They were usually accompanied by jugglers, acrobats, and other performers, and all kept time to marching music provided by musicians playing trumpets, flutes, drums, and sometimes a large hydraulic organ. (The organ probably also played during the actual fighting, producing the same effect as the background musical score of a movie.)

Following the *pompa*, the acrobats and other minor performers exited and the gladiators proceeded, in full public view, to draw lots, which decided who would fight whom. Then an official inspected their weapons to make sure they were sound and well-sharpened. Finally, the gladiators soberly raised their weapons toward the highest-ranking official present (usually either the emperor or *munerarius*, the magistrate in charge of the spectacle) and recited the phrase, "*Morituri te salutamus!*" ("We who are about to die salute you!") After that, the first pairing began. Having no rules or referees, the combat was invariably desperate and often savage. The spectators, like those at modern boxing matches and bullfights, reacted excitedly. Typical shouted phrases included "*Verbera!*" ("Strike!"), "*Habet!*" ("A hit!"), "*Hoc habet!*" ("Now he's done for!"), and "*Ure!*" ("Burn him up!").

The fighting had several possible outcomes. If both warriors fought bravely and could not best each other, the *munerarius* declared the bout a draw and allowed them to leave the arena and fight another day. Sometimes both officials and spectators felt that the fighters were not giving it their all. Or one man turned and ran. "Officiosus fled on November 6 in the consulate of Drusus Caesar and M. Junius Norbanus,"[75] reads a Pompeiian inscription. Such offenders were punished by whipping or branding with hot irons.

A more common outcome was when one gladiator went down wounded. He was allowed to raise one finger, a sign of appeal for mercy, after which the emperor or *munerarius* decided his fate, usually in accordance with the crowd's wishes. If the spectators desired a fighter spared, they either waved their handkerchiefs or pointed their thumbs downward, the signal for the victor to drop his or her sword. At the same time they shouted "*Mitte!*" ("Spare him!") On the other hand, if the choice was death, they pressed their thumbs toward their own chests (symbolizing a sword through the heart) and yelled "*Iugula!*" ("Cut his throat!").

Another possible outcome was when one fighter killed an opponent outright;

and still another when the fallen combatant pretended to be dead. Few, if any, were successful at this ruse, for men dressed like the Etruscan demon Charun (a retained custom illustrating the games' Etruscan roots) ran out and applied hot irons to the bodies. Any fakers exposed in this way promptly had their throats cut. Then young boys cleaned the blood stains from the sand, and men dressed as the god Mercury (transporter of the dead) whisked away the corpses, all in preparation for the next round of battles.

Animal Hunts and Pitiless Slaughter

Gladiators were not the only popular attractions in the arena spectacles. There were also ferocious fights between humans and beasts and between beasts and beasts, generally termed *venationes*, or "hunts." Originally they were minor spectacles presented mainly in early morning before the bulk of the spectators had arrived. By the early Empire, however, the hunts had become popular enough to warrant staging them in late afternoon, when more people attended arena shows. Noted classical historian Lionel Casson provides this summary of the hunts:

> At vast expense the Roman government imported animals from every corner of the known world—tigers from India, leopards from Asia Minor, lions and elephants and other creatures from Africa, wild bulls from northern Europe, and so on. They were kept in cages under the arena until, at the appropriate moment, they

Gladiators in the Movies

Unfortunately, few film depictions of ancient Roman gladiatorial combats have been accurately costumed or staged. One notable exception was *Spartacus* (1960, directed by Stanley Kubrick).

In the film, the title character (played by Kirk Douglas) is the real-life slave who led a huge slave rebellion against the Roman state in the first century B.C. Before escaping the gladiator school to which he was brought in chains, he is forced to fight a fellow trainee in a small arena to gratify a group of Roman aristocrats who are visiting the school. Spartacus is arrayed as a Thracian, with an exposed chest, small round shield (*parma*), and curved sword (*sica*), while his opponent is a *retiarius*. Although the latter defeats Spartacus in the duel, he refuses to slay the fallen man and soon suffers death for his insolence. This scene impressively recreates the spectacle, excitement, and brutality of the Roman arena.

This is a shot from the scene described above, in which Spartacus (played by Kirk Douglas), a Thracian gladiator, fights a retiarius *(in foreground with trident).*

were brought up and let loose. As they wandered about, crazed or dazed, *bestiarii*, "beast men," low-level gladiators trained for this sort of thing, stepped in against them with knife and spear; the *bestiarius* had a chance of surviving, the animals none. Or crack native hunters were sent in to cut them down ruthlessly with bow and arrow or javelin—which at least added some dimension of skill to the carnage.[76]

The gruesome toll of animals butchered in this manner must have been enormous. The record of 9,000 beasts slaughtered during the 100 days of the emperor Titus's inauguration of the Colosseum in A.D. 80 was surpassed in 107 when the emperor Trajan presented immense spectacles lasting 123 days. At least 11,000 animals were killed in these games. In the nearly four centuries in which this and other amphitheaters housed such shows, millions of animals likely met their doom. And all the while, the crowds cheered on the hunters, who occasionally became almost as popular as winning gladiators. The first-century A.D. Roman poet Martial left behind this glowing praise for the hunter Carpophorus, who gained fame in the arena during Domitian's reign (A.D. 81–96):

> He plunged his hunter's spear also in a headlong-rushing bear, the king of beasts beneath the cope of Arctic skies; and he laid low a lion, magnificent, of bulk unknown before, one worthy of Hercules' might; and with a far-dealt wound stretched in death a rushing leopard. He won the prize of honor; yet unbroken still was his strength.[77]

Some hunters specialized in killing one kind of animal, like the *taurarii*, who,

much like modern matadors, confronted bulls and attempted to stab them with lances. An exciting variation resembled a modern rodeo event; a man jumped from horseback onto the bull, grabbed its horns, and tried to wrestle it to the ground. In a strange juxtaposition of pitiless slaughter and charming frivolity, a *venatio* usually concluded with some comic relief in the form of trained animal acts like those in today's circuses.

Massacres and Naval Battles

Meanwhile, interspersed with the periodic slaughter of nearly helpless animals were shows featuring the massacre of *completely* helpless humans. While various kinds of petty criminals might be sentenced to the gladiator schools, many of the most serious offenders were condemned to outright execution in the arena. This was certainly not sport by any modern definition of the word; yet, as an ever-present component of the general spectacle that the Romans viewed as sport, it cannot be ignored. The *munerarius* took charge of the condemned men, guaranteeing that each would be killed within a year. Usually at around noon, before the formal gladiatorial bouts had begun, guards herded the unarmed criminals up onto the arena floor, where some were quickly hacked down by a troop of fully armed gladiators. Others were crucified, and still others tied to stakes, on which they were mangled and eaten by half-starved lions, bears, and other beasts. Often during these massacres, attendants veiled any emperors' statues adorning the amphitheater, symbolically sparing them the sight of

This bust purportedly depicts Seneca, Nero's tutor and a noted playwright and Stoic philosopher, whose comments about death in the arena are often quoted.

and often repeated. Caesar staged a *naumachia* in 46 B.C., and Augustus held one of the most impressive on record in 2 B.C. Augustus later bragged:

> I presented to the people an exhibition of a naval battle across the Tiber [River] where a grove of the Caesars now is, having had the site excavated 1,800 feet [about 549 meters] in length and 1,200 feet [about 366 meters] in width. In this exhibition thirty beaked ships [i.e., equipped with rams], triremes [ships with three banks of oars] or biremes [with two banks], and in addition a great number of smaller vessels engaged in combat. On board these fleets, exclusive of rowers, there were about 3,000 combatants.[78]

"It Was Pure Murder"

The fact that the spectators found all this bloodshed and death entertaining has given rise to a common modern conception that most Romans were highly insensitive and/or cruel. But this is a simplistic, misleading, and distorted view of the Roman character. For one thing, some Romans, particularly better-educated ones, found the bloodletting of the arena distasteful, even when the participants were hardened criminals. For example, Seneca, the brilliant philosopher and writer who counseled Nero for some years, expressed his disdain at the slaughter of a group of unarmed condemned men:

> I happened on the noon interlude at the arena, expecting some clever burlesque, some relaxation to give the spectators a respite [break] from

"riff-raff" in their death throes. Supposedly the emperor Claudius (reigned A.D. 41–54) ordered so many executions that he had a statue of Augustus removed so it would not have to be constantly veiled.

Criminals (along with war prisoners) also died in staged naval battles known as *naumachia*. In the roles of sailors and soldiers in rival fleets, they fought to the death in full-sized ships, usually on lakes or in special basins (also called *naumachia*) dug to accommodate these spectacles. Often the men were outfitted to represent the participants of famous historical naval battles; the Greek-Persian encounter at Salamis (480 B.C.) was particularly popular

Christians Die in the Arena?

Although firm documented evidence is lacking, it is likely that some early Christians were among the victims mauled by lions, bears, and other wild animals in the Roman games. According to tradition, the first Christian who died in the Colosseum was Saint Ignatius, bishop of Antioch, the first writer to refer to the church as "catholic," or universal. Supposedly, he welcomed martyrdom in the arena and exclaimed shortly before his death, "I am as the grain of the field, and must be ground by the teeth of the lions, that I may become fit for His [God's] table."

It should be noted, however, that the popular notion that the Romans were religiously intolerant and persecuted the Christians for having different beliefs is mistaken. By the mid–first century A.D., when Christianity was first spreading through the Empire, the highly tolerant Romans had welcomed and themselves practiced numerous alternative and often exotic religions from around the Mediterranean world. All of these flourished alongside Rome's state religion, which venerated traditional gods like Jupiter, Juno, and Minerva.

What made the early Christians different was their own intolerance. In addition to condemning all other beliefs but their own, many of them refused to acknowledge the emperor's authority, which disturbed the traditionally highly

patriotic Romans. Moreover, the Christians kept to themselves, appearing to be antisocial, and over time they acquired the terrible stigma of having *odium generis humani*, a "hatred for the human race." Worst of all, unfounded rumors spread that Christian rituals included cannibalism, incest, and other repugnant acts. Most Romans came to believe these fables and therefore felt little or no pity for any of the Christians who may have suffered torment and death on the arena's blood-soaked sands.

In this nineteenth-century woodcut, a Christian woman meets a grisly fate before the gaze of thousands in a Roman arena.

human gore. [But] the show was the reverse. The fighting that had gone before was charity by contrast. Now there was no nonsense about it; it was pure murder. The men have nothing to protect them; the whole body is exposed and every stroke tells. Many spectators prefer this to the usual matches. Why shouldn't they? There is no helmet or shield to parry the steel. Why armor? Why skill? Such things [merely] delay the [inevitable] kill.[79]

Cicero had less concern for condemned people receiving "their just rewards," but felt genuine pity for the wholesale killing of beasts by men and men by beasts. "What pleasure can a civilized man find," he asked, "when either a helpless human being is mangled by a very strong animal, or a magnificent animal is stabbed again and again with a hunting spear?"[80] Sharing these feelings was the second-century A.D. emperor Marcus Aurelius, who thoroughly disliked the butchery of both humans and beasts. Attending the Colosseum strictly out of a sense of duty to his subjects, he ignored the games and utilized the time dictating letters and conducting other state business.

The supremely educated Seneca, Cicero, and Aurelius were in the minority; most Romans found the arena's spectacles of bloodletting fascinating and entertaining. But before this attitude is automatically condemned as inhumane, the fact that it evolved in a culture with traditions and beliefs very different from our own must be considered. The *munera* and other bloody sporting spectacles constituted the outward expression of emotions, feelings, and principles deeply ingrained in the Roman character. On the one hand, the Romans had a powerful superstitious awe and fascination for death and all the trappings that accompanied it. In watching other living things die, many experienced a temporary emotional release from their own terror of dying.

A Societal Double Standard

On the other hand, Roman fascination with gladiators was bound up in large degree with an obsessive and seemingly contradictory form of hero worship. Socially speaking, gladiators were considered crude, worthless, and undignified lowlifes. Like actors and other entertainers, arena fighters bore the degrading stigma of *infamia* ("bad reputation" or "outcast"). Yet at the same time, gladiators who won often became popular heroes on par with today's biggest football, baseball, and basketball stars. Moreover, the Romans perceived in a gladiator's sacrifice of blood a sadly tragic but still heroic figure to be admired and honored. The gladiator took a solemn oath that he (or she) would die, without hesitation, for his audience of "betters." Such an act of complete and ultimate submission to the will of one's "master" made the gladiator, in Roman eyes, a model for a person of honor. "Consider the blows they endure!" Cicero exclaimed in a powerfully worded passage.

Consider how they who have been well-disciplined prefer to accept a blow than shamefully avoid it! How often it is made clear that they consider nothing other than the satisfaction of their master or the people! Even when they are covered with wounds they send a mes-

Gladiators march into the Colosseum during the colorful opening ceremony known as the pompa. *Inevitably, some will not march out.*

senger to their master to inquire his will. If they have given satisfaction to their masters, they are pleased to fall. What even mediocre gladiator ever groans, ever alters the expression on his face? Which one of them acts shamefully either standing or falling? And which of them, even when he does succumb, ever contracts his neck when ordered to receive the [death] blow?[81]

Thus, the Romans maintained an odd societal double standard about gladiators and other arena fighters. This strongly felt "love-hate" relationship, along with various other deeply rooted religious and ethical traditions and beliefs, made the spectacle of death in the arena highly compelling to Roman audiences.

Part of Rome's unique catalog of violent sporting events, such spectacles became as integral to everyday Roman life as baseball is to modern American life. "The spectacle was awaited with impatience," writes Roland Auguet, a noted authority on Roman games.

> Everyone discussed it, some applauded and others booed frantically. Goaded by habit, by idleness, by fanaticism, an entire people crowded onto the tiers of the . . . amphitheater, as to a temple which had a ritual peculiar to it. In Rome there was undoubtedly an emotion special to the amphitheater, even as there exists among us a quite special pleasure on entering a cinema, regardless of the film which is to be shown.[82]

Imagine, therefore, the air of excitement that rippled through Pompeii after the following advertisement appeared one morning, freshly painted on a wall: "The gladiatorial troop hired by Aulus Suettius Certus will fight in Pompeii on May 31. There will also be a wild animal hunt. The awnings [a canvas to keep out rain] will be used."[83]

Chapter

5 "He Came from Behind to Win": Horse and Chariot Racing

For both Greeks and Romans, the equestrian events—horse and chariot racing—were among the oldest and most popular sports. These events came first on the program, amid much pomp and circumstance, at the ancient Olympics and many other Greek games. And in Rome, attending the chariot races became far and away the most popular pastime. On each of the roughly 17 days a year that races were held in Rome during the early Empire, upwards of 250,000 people, perhaps a quarter of the city's population, crowded in and around the huge racetrack, the Circus Maximus.

The exact origins of equestrian sports are unknown. During the late second and early first millennia B.C., royal and aristocratic houses across western Asia and southern Europe raised horses and often used both horses and chariots in warfare. During these centuries events demonstrating equestrian skills were incorporated into the games accompanying religious festivals. The Greeks and Etruscans were racing chariots at least as early as the 700s B.C., and probably earlier, as the descriptions of such races in the *Iliad* suggest. Both peoples were likely influenced by the early cultures of Asia Minor, an area with an ancient tradition of horse breeding and chariot making.

The Greeks and Etruscans, who had splendid cities in Italy when Rome was still a backward little town, probably introduced horse racing to the Romans. According to a later Roman story, shortly after establishing Rome in 753 B.C., the legendary Romulus held chariot races, to which he invited a neighboring people, the Sabines.[84] However, even if the Romans did hold races this early, they were undoubtedly small, infrequent affairs; it took several more centuries for racing to develop into a large-scale institution in Rome.

By contrast, chariot racing was well established in Greek games by the seventh century B.C. The Olympic Games, for example, first ran the four-horse race, the *tethrippon*, in 680 B.C. No one knows the actual circumstances surrounding the introduction of the event, but the Greeks had a charming legend about it. Supposedly Oinomaos, king of Pisa, a district near Elis, had a daughter, Hippodameia, whose hand in marriage many young men sought. The king agreed to allow any suitor to marry his daughter providing the young man could drive his own chariot faster than the king's. If the king caught up, he would hurl his javelin, killing the suitor. This scenario played out time and again, until many prospective bridegrooms lay dead in the dust. Then the young champion Pelops ar-

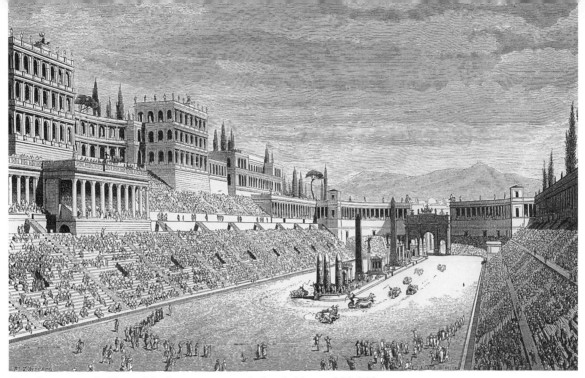

Rome's mammoth Circus Maximus, a racetrack that held over 200,000 spectators, comes to life in this modern reconstruction. The central island is called the spina.

rived to try his luck. The god Poseidon, who favored Pelops over Oinomaos, gave the young man a golden chariot with four winged horses, which easily outdistanced the team driven by the king, who fell from his own chariot and died. This contest purportedly inspired the introduction of formal races at local festivals, beginning with the one at Olympia.

Greek Racetracks

However they began, Greek equestrian events took place on a track called a hippodrome. Unlike later Roman circuses, which were large stone facilities with tiers of seats for spectators, Greek hippodromes were essentially open fields lined with raised banks of earth, on which the spectators stood. The one at Olympia covered a space about 250 meters (820 feet) wide and about 399 meters (1,310 feet) long. Pausanias's description of it, the only surviving ancient account of a Greek hippodrome, mentions, among other things, the starting gates and a turning post:

> If you climb out of the stadium near where the Greek judges sit, you come to an area where the ground has been leveled for horse-racing and to the starting-place for horses. The starting-place is shaped like the prow of a ship, with the beak pointed towards the race-course. . . . Each of the sides is over four hundred feet [122 meters] long. . . . Instead of an automatic cable they use a rope stretched in front of

In this ruined hippodrome in Tyre (on the coast of Palestine), the remains of the starting gates can be seen in the distance at left.

the chariots or the race-horses. . . . The clerk of the course operates the machinery. . . . The first cables to give are the ones on both sides . . . and the horses in those positions gallop out first, and as they gallop past the horses in the second position the cables give in the second position as well, and the same thing happens with all the horses until they are even at the beak of the prow, and from then on it is all a matter of the experience of the drivers and the speed of the horses. . . . One side of the race-course is longer than the other, and on the longer side, which is a mound . . . is the terror of horses, the "horse-scarer." The shape is like a circular altar, and as horses gallop past it they suffer extreme panic from no visible cause. The panic puts them into confusion, the chariots are smashed up, and the drivers are injured. . . . On one of the turning-posts is a bronze portrait of Hippodameia [from the legend] holding a ribbon to tie on Pelops's head as the winner.[85]

The triangular starting gate that Pausanias describes apparently had stalls for the individual horses or chariots set at intervals along its long sides. This allowed for a staggered start, without which there would have been no room to line up the contestants side by side, since Greek races had thirty or forty, and perhaps sometimes as many as sixty, entrants. The "horse-scarer" was an altar set up on one end of the track; but why it frightened the horses is unclear. One of the explanations Pausanias passed on was that the ghost of one of the young suitors killed by Oinomaos haunted the altar and leapt out at the animals as they passed by. One of the more likely recent explanations is that horses nearing the altar faced the rising sun, which temporarily blinded and confused them.

The turn near the altar was not the only dangerous aspect of a race in the hippodrome. The contest's grueling length (the *tethrippon* was over thirteen kilometers, or eight miles, long) and the large number of competitors weaving in, out, and around one another as they sparred for advantage must have made crashes and spills fairly routine. Pindar mentions a race at Delphi in which forty chariots crashed.[86] This excerpt from *Electra*, by the fifth-century B.C. Athenian playwright Sophocles, depicts an exciting series of collisions:

> To begin with, all went well with every chariot. Then the Aenian's tough colts took the bit in their teeth and on the turn from the sixth to the seventh lap, ran head-on into the African. The accident led to other upsets and collisions, till the field . . . was a sea of wrecked and capsized chariots. The Athenian driver had seen what was coming and was clever enough to draw aside and bide his time while the oncoming wave crashed into inextricable confusion. Orestes was driving past, purposely holding his team back and pinning his faith to the final spurt; and now, seeing only one rival left in, with an exultant shout to his swift horses he drove hard ahead and the two teams raced neck and neck, now one now the other gaining a lead. . . . But at the last [lap], Orestes misjudged the turn, slackened his left rein before the horse was safely round the bend, and so fouled the [turning] post. The hub was smashed across, and he was hurled over the rail entangled in the severed reins, and as he fell his horses ran wild across the course.[87]

Jockeys and Owners

The Greeks eventually added other equestrian events besides the four-horse chariot race to their games. A two-horse chariot event, the *synoris*, entered the program at Olympia in 408 B.C. A mule-cart race was

This bronze statue of a jockey atop a steed (now on display in Athens) captures the grace and fluidity of man and beast working in unison. It also shows that Greek jockeys rode bareback, which was both difficult and dangerous.

added in 500 B.C. but was dropped about a half-century later, perhaps because the Eleans did not like it.[88] The *calpe*, a race in which the rider dismounted at the start of the final lap and ran the rest of the way on foot, was introduced in 496 B.C. For reasons that are unclear, this event was deleted the same year the mule-cart contest was.

The regular horse race, in which a jockey rode on a horse's back, first appeared in the Olympic program in 648 B.C. Today's jockeys require a great deal of skill and face a moderate risk of falling. By comparison, ancient Greek horse racing was a far more difficult and dangerous sport, partly because the riders lacked the benefits of certain basic pieces of equipment that modern jockeys take for granted. The saddle, horseshoes, stirrups, and horse collar were all unknown to the Greeks and Romans. Without the protection and stability afforded by saddle and stirrups, a rider had great difficulty staying on the animal and often suffered injuries to the genitals and kidneys. The harness the Greeks employed choked the horse when the rider pulled on the reins, impeding the beast's performance. And having no shoes, the horses could not get a good grip on the ground. Complicating this problem was the fact that the horse race directly followed the chariot races; so the jockeys and their mounts had to race on a course that was already badly churned and rutted. Needless to say, any rider who made it all the way to the finish line, much less won, deserved to be called a great athlete.

Such charioteers and riders did not receive the recognition that runners, wrestlers, and other athletes did, however. This was because it was not they, but the owners of the horses and teams, who were awarded the victory prizes. The drivers and riders, who could be either slaves or free persons, were usually just hired hands.[89] As remains true today, it was expensive to keep and train horses, so the well-to-do generally controlled the sport. Some fans evidently became totally absorbed in the races. In his play *Clouds*, Aristophanes pokes fun at such characters in his portrayal of a race-addicted young man who dreams of horses in his sleep and whose huge expenditures on them are driving his rich father toward bankruptcy. Sometimes, for propaganda purposes, a city-state financed a chariot team, as when a "public chariot" from Argos won at Olympia in 472 B.C.

Interestingly, ownership of horses and chariot teams afforded women their only means of competing in the Olympics. They could not participate directly by driving or riding, of course, but if their horses or teams won, they received the prizes and the glory. Twice, for example, in 396 and 392 B.C., Kyniska, the daughter of a Spartan king, won the Olympic chariot race. "My ancestors and my brothers were kings," she boasted. "I, Kyniska, won the chariot race with my swift-footed horses and erected this statue."[90] Several other Greek women won similar honors at Olympia and elsewhere.

The Roman Charioteers

Unlike Greek charioteers, their Roman counterparts often became widely popular sports figures, which constituted one of the principal differences between Greek and Roman racing. Many, if not most, Roman charioteers began as slaves and rarely gained true social acceptance in polite society, which always looked on entertaining

The victor of a Roman chariot race comes charging around the end of the spina *in this modern rendering. His four-horse vehicle is called a* quadrigarum.

as a degrading profession.[91] Yet, like successful gladiators, winning racers were widely admired among the general populace. Some charioteers became "like movie stars today," University of California scholar Jo-Ann Shelton points out, "recognized as they walked down the streets of Rome and greeted with swoons and squeals of delight."[92]

Although the owners of horses and teams received the purse money, they gave their drivers monetary rewards; and successful charioteers eventually gained their freedom (if they started out as slaves) and began receiving hefty percentages of the purse. Thus, it was not uncommon for popular drivers to become rich men. According to Juvenal, "You'll find that a hundred lawyers scarcely make more than one successful jockey."[93] And as Martial complained, "How long among the milling, toga'ed throng of parasites must I, for a whole day's work, bring back the worthless dole [government handouts], when Scorpus in his chariot gets fifteen sacks of gold, mint-hot, in an hour?"[94]

Scorpus, who won over 2,000 races and died in a track accident at age 26, was only one of many successful racers mentioned in ancient writings or inscriptions. The inscription on a monument erected by one of them, Calpurnianus, tells how he won 1,127 victories, including several that paid him 40,000 *sestercii* (about 40 times the annual wage of an average Roman soldier) or more. Another popular charioteer, Crescens, began racing at age 13 and died at age 24, earning over 1.5 million *sestercii* in his short but glorious career. One of the most remarkable records was that of Diocles, who also set up his own monument, recording the following facts for posterity:

> He drove four-horse chariots for 24 years. He had 4,257 starts, with 1,462 first-place finishes, 110 of them in opening races [several races were held each day]. In single-entry races, he had 1,064 first-place finishes, winning 92 major purses, 32 of them worth 30,000 *sestercii* . . . 28 of them worth 40,000 *sestercii* . . . 29 worth 50,000 *sestercii* . . . and three worth 60,000 *sestercii*. . . . All total, he was in the money 2,900 times. . . . In races for two-horse chariots, he had 3 first-place finishes. . . . In 815 races, he took the lead at the start and held it to the end. In 67 races, he came from behind to win.[95]

"A Meeting Place for the Roman World"

Diocles' inscription shows that he won most of his victories on four-horse chariots. Called *quadrigae*, these were the most common races. He also mentions competing occasionally in two-horse versions (*bigae*). Less frequently seen, although not rare, were races for chariots with three horses (*trigae*), six (*seiuges*), eight (*octoiuges*), and even ten (*decemiuges*). Another race staged only occasionally was the *pedibus ad quadrigam*, in which two men stood in the chariot; when the vehicle crossed the finish line, one of them jumped out and sprinted once around the course.

Roman racing featured no regular horse races (with a jockey riding a horse), as did Greek racing, marking another important difference between the two equestrian traditions. The nearest Roman equivalent were the *desultorii*, who probably entertained the crowds in the intervals between the chariot races. More of an acrobat than a rider, a *desultor* stood on the backs of two horses that were reined together and performed various jumps and tricks.

The kind of tracks on which these races and performances took place constituted another major difference between Greek and Roman racing styles. Greek hippodromes were, for the most part, open spaces in the countryside; the Romans, meanwhile, erected large stadiumlike structures, called circuses, usually in or around urban areas. Several dozen circuses dotted the Empire by the second century A.D. Rome itself eventually had four, including the largest ever built—the Circus Maximus.[96] Begun in the early Republic and expanded and improved over the centuries, this facility became one of the architectural marvels of the ancient world. It was about half a kilometer (over a third of a mile) long and almost 153 meters (500 feet) wide. Running lengthwise down the middle was the central axis, the *euripus* (or *spina*), decorated with statues and obelisks, around which the chariots raced. On the days when it featured races, the Great Circus, as it was often called, presented perhaps twenty-four races in a day by the A.D. 40s.

The crowds who jammed the circuses to watch these races were a mix of men, women, freedmen (freed slaves), and slaves, for anyone who could find a place to sit or stand could attend, and admission was free. Because they often watched for many hours at a stretch, spectators often sat on cushions, either carried from home or rented at the circus. They also periodically gorged themselves on fast food provided by roving vendors or snack bars located beneath the stands. Besides the spectators and merchants, prostitutes, gamblers, pickpockets, and others roamed through the facility, so that it was, as Robert Kebric memorably puts it, "literally a meeting place for the Roman world."[97] The following passage by the first-century B.C. Roman poet Ovid shows that a race was as much a social occasion as it was a sporting spectacle.

I'm not sitting here because of my enthusiasm for horse races; but I will pray that the chariot driver you favor may win. I came here, in fact, so that I might sit beside you and talk to you. I didn't want the love which you stir in me to be concealed from you. So, you watch the races, and I'll watch you. Let's each watch the things we love most, and let's feast our eyes on them. . . . Why are you edging away from me? It's no use. The seat marker forces us to touch. Yes, the Circus does offer some advantages in its seating rules. Hey, you on the right, whoever you are, be more considerate of the lady! . . . Draw in your legs, if you have any sense of decency, and don't stick your bony knees in her back. Oh dear, your skirt is trailing a bit on the ground. Lift it up, or here, I will do it. . . . Would you

These ruins are part of what little is left of the great Circus Maximus. A meeting place for Romans of all walks of life, the facility featured not only chariot races, but also a festive social atmosphere.

Dimensions of the Great Circus

This description of Rome's mammoth Circus Maximus is from the informative book Roman People, *by historian Robert B. Kebric of the University of Louisville.*

"The Circus was immense by any standard. Externally, its length was about 680 yards [622 meters] (over a third of a mile), while its width was 150 yards [137 meters]. The most recent estimates place its seating capacity at about 150,000, although some ancient sources make it 250,000 and more. It is difficult to reconcile this discrepancy. . . . The Romans were notorious for overcrowding, and we can never know how many people they actually packed into the Circus. . . . The ancient figures may have included those who watched from the hills overlooking the track. . . . The arena of the Circus measured about 635 by 85 yards [582 by 78 meters], or roughly twelve times that of the Colosseum, another of Rome's great spectator facilities. Its floor was a bed of compacted earth covered with a layer of sand, designed to allow the chariots to hold the track (especially on the turns), to save the horses from injury, and to drain off water. . . . At one end of the Circus were twelve starting gates (*carceres*). Running down the middle of the arena, closer to the rounded end of the facility, was a long, narrow barrier (frequently identified as the *spina* but more accurately called the *euripus*). Approximately 365 yards [334 meters] in length, it was covered with an assortment of shrines, altars, and other monuments, including two large obelisks brought from Egypt. It was around this barrier, which had turning posts (*metae*) at each end, that the chariots whirled seven death-defying times (about 3 miles) [or about 5 kilometers], always to the driver's left. Seven large bronze dolphins at one end of the barrier and seven 'eggs' at the other end were used to indicate the lap number. . . . Since a bronze dolphin was part of the starting mechanism at the Hippodrome in Olympia, where the Olympic Games were held, the Circus's dolphins may also have provided a link with the older tradition of horse racing in Greece."

This modern drawing captures the thrill of excitement that rippled through the stands during a chariot race. Roman racing fans backed various factions (clubs or organizations), each represented by a specific color, much as modern sports fans cheer for their home teams.

like me to stir a light breeze by using my program as a fan? . . . Good, the track is clear and ready for the first big race. . . . I can see the driver you're cheering for. I'm sure he'll win. . . . Oh no, he's swinging wide around the turning post. What are you doing? The driver in second position is coming up from behind. . . . Oh, we're cheering for an idiot and a coward. . . . The starting gates are open again, the horses break, and the different-colored teams fly onto the track. Now, gallop ahead and take a clear lead! Fulfill my girlfriend's hopes, and my own.[98]

Of Factions and Fanatical Fans

Ovid's mention of "different-colored teams" is a reference to rival racing organizations, or factions, each identified by the color of the tunics its drivers wore. In some ways they were similar to modern professional sports teams, which often have their own traditional rivalries. In the late Republic, there were only two factions—the Whites and the Reds; the Blues and Greens appeared in the first century A.D.[99] In time, having four factions proved unpopular with the populace, and by the mid–second century or so the Blues had absorbed the Reds and the Greens the Whites. From then on, for the rest of Rome's history, the Blues and Greens battled for the allegiance of racing fans.

Such fan allegiance for the factions was often intense, even fanatical, as it is today among the supporters of national soccer teams at the World Cup competitions. In a letter to a friend, the first-century A.D. diplomat and writer Pliny the Younger, who held himself intellectually above the "childish passions" of the racing scene, commented on such zealous devotion to colors:

If they [the fans] were attracted by the speed of the horses or the drivers' skill one could account for it, but in fact it is the racing-colors they really support and care about, and if the colors were to be exchanged in mid–course during a race, they would transfer their favor and enthusiasm and rapidly desert the famous drivers and horses whose names they shout as they recognize them from afar. Such is the popularity of a worthless shirt—I don't mean with the crowd, which is worth less than the shirt, but with certain serious individuals. When I think of how this futile, tedious, monotonous business can keep them sitting endlessly in their seats, I take pleasure in the fact that their pleasure is not mine.[100]

As usual, Juvenal made the same point more humorously. Here, he compares fan reaction to a team's loss to the aftermath of the Battle of Cannae, the worst military defeat Rome ever suffered:

If I may say so without offense to that countless mob, all Rome is in the Circus today. The roar that assails my eardrums means, I am pretty sure, that the Greens have won—otherwise you'd see such gloomy faces, such sheer astonishment as greeted the Cannae disaster, after our consuls [administrator-generals] had bitten the dust.[101]

Later, in the sixth century, rivalry between the Blues and Greens became so fanatical in Constantinople (Rome's eastern capital, which had survived the fall of the western Empire) that their supporters routinely attacked and killed one another. When the emperor Justinian tried to stem the violence by arresting several faction leaders, it touched off a riot that almost destroyed the city.

Thrills and Spills on the Racetrack

Such team rivalry was most intense and dangerous on the racetrack itself, of course. A Roman poet, Sidonius Apollinaris, left behind the most detailed and vivid ancient account of a Roman chariot race, in which his friend, Consentius, competed:

The four team colors are clearly visible: white and blue, green and red. . . . A shrill blast of the trumpet, and the chariots leap out of the gates, onto the track. . . . The wheels fly over the ground, and the air is choked with the dust stirred up on the track. . . . The chariots fly out of sight [i.e., behind the *euripus*], quickly covering the long open stretch. . . . When they have come around the far turn . . . the rival teams have passed Consentius, but his partner is in the lead. The middle teams concentrate now on taking the lead in the inside lane. . . . Consentius, however, redoubles his efforts to hold back his horses and skillfully reserve their energy for the seventh and last lap. The others race full out, urging their horses with whip and voice. . . . And thus they race, the first lap, the second, the third, the fourth. In the fifth lap the leader is no longer able to withstand the pressure of his pursuers. . . . When the sixth lap had been completed . . . Consentius's opponents thought they had a very safe lead for the seventh and last lap. . . . But suddenly he loosens the reins, plants his feet firmly on the floorboard, leans far over the chariot. . . and makes his fast

Racing Rivalries Lead to Rioting

In this excerpt from his classic book History of the Later Roman Empire, *the late, distinguished historian J. B. Bury tells how rivalry among racing fans in Constantinople led to rioting and the slaughter of thousands of people.*

"The famous rising at Constantinople, which occurred in the first month of A.D. 532 and wrecked the city. . . began with a riot of the Hippodrome factions. . . . Immediately after his accession, [the new emperor Justinian] laid injunctions on the authorities in every city that the disorders and crime of the factions should be punished impartially. A number of persons belonging to both factions had been arrested for a riot in which there had been loss of life. . . . The Prefect of the City . . . condemned four to be beheaded and three to be hanged. But in the case of two, the hangman blundered and twice the bodies fell, still alive, to the ground. . . . The ides of January fell three days later . . . and according to custom, horse races were held in the Hippodrome, and the emperor was present. Both the Blues and the Greens importuned the emperor . . . to show mercy to the two culprits who had been rescued by accident from the gallows. No answer was accorded, and at the twenty-second race [the cry arose] 'Long live the humane Greens and Blues!' The cry announced that the two parties would act in concert to force the government to grant a pardon. . . . When the races were over, the factions agreed on a watchword, *nika*, "conquer," and the rising which followed was known as the Nika Revolt. . . . The rioters broke into the prison, released the criminals who were confined in it, killed some of the officials, and set fire to the building. . . . They fired the . . . entrance of the Great Palace, and not only was this consumed, but the flames spread northward to the Senate-house and the church of St. Sophia. These buildings were burned down. . . . The insurgents crowded the [Hippodrome] in dense masses, and reviled [denounced] Justinian. . . . [Justinian was now advised] to attack the people crowded in the Hippodrome. . . . They were cut down without mercy, and . . . it was said that the number of the slain exceeded 30,000."

This chariot-racing scene, with its crashes and cheering fans, is reminiscent of those depicted in the 1880 novel Ben-Hur, *by Lew Wallace, and the two film versions made from it in 1926 and 1959.*

horses gallop full out. One of the other drivers tries to make a very sharp turn at the far post . . . but he is unable to turn his four wildly excited horses, and they plunge out of control. Consentius passes him carefully. The fourth driver . . . turns his galloping horses too far right toward the stands. Consentius drives straight and fast and passes [him]. . . . The latter pursues Consentius recklessly, hoping to overtake him. He cuts in sharply across the track. His horses lose their balance and fall. Their legs become tangled in the spinning chariot wheels and are snapped and broken. The driver is hurled headlong out of the shattered chariot which then falls on top of him in a heap of twisted wreckage. . . . And now the emperor presents the palm branch of victory to Consentius.[102]

This account undoubtedly provided American writer Lew Wallace with much of his inspiration for the great chariot race he depicted in his famous 1880 novel, *Ben-Hur*. The book was itself the inspiration for two spectacular films (released in 1926 and 1959). In a way then, via the on-screen exploits of Wallace's charioteers, Consentius and his opponents still live on, repeatedly recapturing the thrills and spills of Rome's favorite sport for eager new generations.

Chapter

6 Of Balls, Beaches, Boats, and Bears: Leisure Sports and Games

The formal, large-scale, public, usually professional games and races featured in the stadiums, hippodromes, amphitheaters, and circuses were not the only sports the Greeks and Romans enjoyed. They also engaged in numerous informal, small-scale, more private, and often (though not exclusively) noncompetitive sportlike activities. Collectively referred to here as leisure sports and games, they included playing ball, swimming, boating, hunting, fishing, mountain climbing, and others.

As people the world over do today, the Greeks and Romans thoroughly enjoyed ball games; and they had many different varieties, which they played in gyms, bath-

houses, private clubs, and, most often, in the streets. There appear to have been three basic kinds of balls. One, the *harpastum*, was small, hard, and stuffed with hair, perhaps like a modern golf ball, only a bit larger. The *pila* was slightly larger and softer, being stuffed with feathers. The other common ball, the *follis*, was an animal bladder (or possibly a leather pouch) filled with air, something like a modern basketball. Unfortunately, evidence concerning the rules and specific moves of most ancient ball games is scant, and scholars still argue over which were team sports, which were individual contests, and exactly how they were played.

Two people toss a pila *back and forth in this modern drawing. Unfortunately, the rules and moves of most ancient ball games remain largely a mystery.*

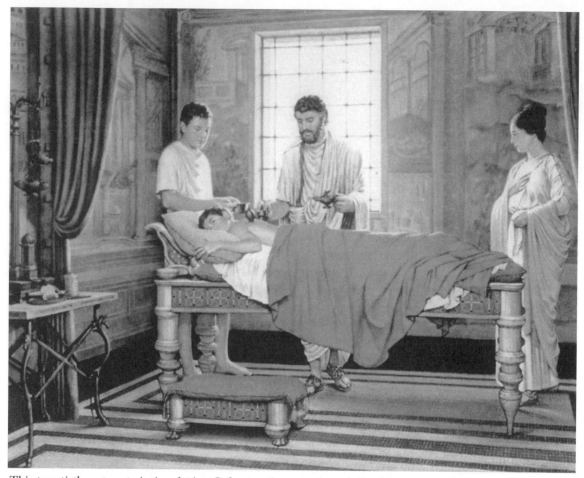

This twentieth-century painting depicts Galen treating a patient. A Greek doctor who made a name for himself in Rome, his writings preserve important information about the sports and games of his day.

One of the simplest and most widely played ball games in the classical world was evidently similar to "keep-away," commonly played in modern grade schools and junior high schools. The difference was that the ancient version was rougher, allowing the players to use headlocks and other wrestling holds. Galen, the renowned second-century A.D. Greek doctor, describes the game, while advocating it as a way to stay in shape, in his treatise titled *Exercise with a Small Ball*:

[The game] is the only one which is so democratic that anyone, no matter how small his income, can take part. You need no nets, no weapons, no horses, no hounds—just a single ball, and a small one at that. . . . The capacity . . . to move all the parts of the body equally . . . is something found in no other exercise except that with a small ball. . . . When for example, people face each other, vigorously attempting to prevent each other from taking the space between, the exercise is a very heavy, vigorous one, involving much use of the hold by the neck, and many wrestling holds. . . . The loins and legs are also subject to great strain in this kind of activity; it requires great steadiness on one's feet.[103]

The game Galen describes here may have been an informal and nonteam variety of one of the most popular of all ancient ball games. A team sport, the Greeks called it *phaininda* and the Romans *harpastum* (suggesting that it employed the small, hard ball of the same name). The second-century A.D. Greek writer Athenaeus left behind this rather vague description of the game:

> He seized the ball and passed it with a laugh to one, while the other player he dodged; from one he pushed it out of the way, while he raised another player to his feet amid resounding shouts of "Out of bounds," "Too far," "Right beside him," "Over his head," "On the ground," "Up in the air," "Too short," "Pass it back."[104]

This passage has led some modern scholars to conclude that *harpastum* was similar to modern rugby (the direct ancestor of American football), which involves kicking, passing, and tackling. Other scholars reject this hypothesis and suggest that another ancient team game, *episkyros*, was closer to rugby. As evidence, they cite this passage by the second-century A.D. Greek scholar Julius Pollux:

> This [game] is played by [two] teams of equal numbers standing opposite one another. They mark out a line between them with stone chips; this is the *skyros* [possibly the scrimmage line], on which the ball is placed. They then mark out two other lines, one behind each team [perhaps goal lines]. The team which secures possession of the ball throws it over their opponents, who then try to get hold of the ball and throw it back, until one side pushes the other over the line behind them. The game might be called a Ball Battle.[105]

Perhaps *harpastum* and *episkyros* were variations of the same game, each with its own unique moves and rules, as is the case with rugby and American football.

Other Ball Games

Martial makes several references to another popular classical ball game, *trigon*, in which three players stood, as if on the points of a triangle, facing one another.[106] Swiftly and deftly, they threw one or more balls back and forth, each attempting not only to catch as many as he could but also to make the others miss. A scorer kept track of the missed balls and apparently the person with the lowest score won.

The Greeks and Romans also had ball games that featured bouncing the ball against a wall, as in modern handball or racquetball. One, which the Romans called *expulsim ludere*, was commonly played by children (and possibly adults, too) in the streets. Others, perhaps along with a more formal version of the street game, utilized specialized courts, known as *sphaeristeria*. Many Roman baths were equipped with these courts, and like many other well-to-do Romans, Pliny the Younger had one in his comfortable villa in Tuscany. "Over the dressing room is built a ball court," he writes, describing the house to a friend, "and this is large enough for several sets of players to take different kinds of exercise."[107]

Private Swimming Pools and Public Beaches

Pliny also makes frequent reference to another popular Greek and Roman pastime—swimming. In the same letter describing his Tuscan villa, he mentions a *piscina*, or swimming pool, this one outdoors and separate from a smaller, colder pool in his private bath. "If you want more space to swim or warmer water," he says, "there is a pool in the courtyard and a well near it to tone you up with cold water when you have had enough of the warm." In another letter, he describes a similar warm pool in his Laurentine villa, this one "much admired [by his guests] and from which swimmers can see the sea."[108] Pre-

sumably, warm pools like Pliny's were heated in the same way as pools in public bathhouses, with a hypocaust, a system of brick conduits that carried hot air generated by a wood-burning furnace.

Not everyone could afford a private pool, of course; but there was plenty of public swimming in rivers, lakes, and at the seaside. Cicero, Ovid, and their renowned contemporary, the poet Horace, all mention swimming in the Tiber, the river flowing past Rome. Horace recommends swimming across the Tiber three times as a cure for insomnia (inability to sleep). In another of his letters, Pliny describes a pleasant Mediterranean beach near the North African Roman town of Hippo:

> People of all ages spend their time here to enjoy the pleasures of fishing, boating, and swimming, especially the boys, who have plenty of time to play. It is a bold feat with them to swim out

A fresco found in an ancient Greek tomb depicts a diver plunging toward the water. Water sports were very popular among both the Greeks and the Romans.

into deep water, the winner being the one who has left the shore and his fellow-swimmers farthest behind.[109]

If not told that it comes from an ancient source, one could easily assume that this is a scene from almost any modern public beach. Similarly, Philostratus left this description of ancient Greek sunbathing:

> Some people take sun baths without giving any thought to the kind of sun or to their own condition; those with experience and good sense do not sunbathe at all times but only when it will be helpful. When the wind comes from the north or when the day is still, the rays of the sun are clean and sunny, since they pass through the bright upper air. When the wind comes from the south or the sky is slightly overcast, the sun's rays are damp and excessively hot, such as to enervate [weaken] those who are training rather than strengthen.[110]

The Greeks and Romans also probably used most of the common swimming strokes used today. A Greek vase now in Paris's Louvre Museum shows a woman using alternate arm strokes, presumably the "crawl," although there is no way to tell whether she is kicking her legs, too. And this passage by a first-century A.D. Roman poet describes a crawl stroke as well as an underwater breast stroke:

> Each person born under the sign of the Dolphin [will] fly through the waves, raising one arm and then the other in slow arcs. At one moment one can hear the sound of the water as he strikes it, at another moment he will separate his arms under water, like an oar concealed by the water.[111]

Boating and Fishing

Pliny mentions boating and fishing, along with swimming, in his Hippo beach scene. Indeed, sailing, rowing, and fishing were leisure sports enjoyed just as much then as they are now. That boating was popular in the classical world is hardly surprising since the Mediterranean has thousands of islands, bays, and inlets, all of them frequented in ancient times by ships of every size and description. The Greek Aegean, with its hundreds of closely spaced isles and warm, clear aqua waters, was a favorite boating area; in Italy, the Gulf of Cumae (now the Bay of Naples), Lake Lucrine, situated just north of the gulf, and the inland lakes near Rome were among the most popular boating areas. As is true today, many well-to-do people owned their own boats, while most other boating enthusiasts rented them. Either way, one seeking to get away from the crowded city, says Martial, could go to pleasant Formiae, on the seacoast south of Rome, where there "is no stagnant sea or air. The deep [water], a living thing, exhales . . . and gently fills the painted sails."[112]

Although most ancient boating seems to have been the kind of leisure pursuit Martial describes, a few ancient sources mention boat races. There appear to have been one or more such races in the Athenian festival games in the fourth century B.C.;[113] and in the same century Alexander the Great staged games in Persia in which teams of rowers and their captains raced warships. In the *Aeneid*, Virgil provides this exciting depiction of the start of a ship race:

> At their helms the captains took their stand in dazzling gold and purple, a

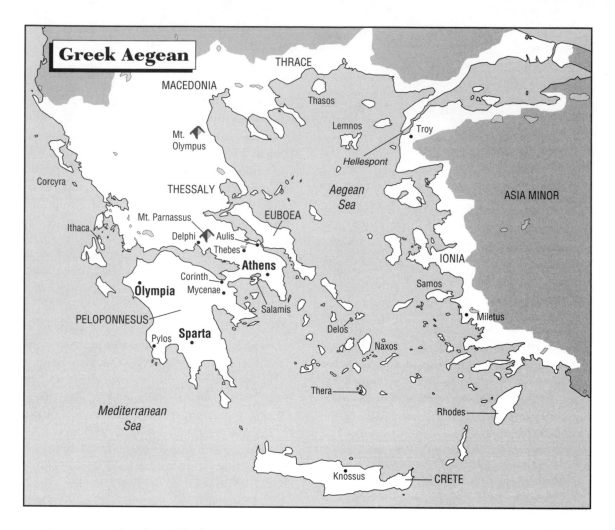

Greek Aegean

THRACE

MACEDONIA

Thasos

Lemnos

Troy

Mt.
Olympus

Hellespont

Corcyra

THESSALY

*Aegean
Sea*

ASIA MINOR

Mt. Parnassus

EUBOEA

Ithaca

Delphi   Aulis

Thebes

Athens

IONIA

Corinth

Olympia

Mycenae

Samos

Miletus

PELOPONNESUS

Salamis

Delos

Sparta

Naxos

Pylos

Thera

Rhodes

*Mediterranean
Sea*

Knossus   CRETE

far-seen splendor. Their crews were crowned with garlands of poplar leaves. . . . They took their place at the thwarts, their muscles tensed [and] tensely they waited the signal, their hearts pounding with nervous fear and longing to be the winners. The trumpet gave the signal. Then in a flash all shot away from the start; and seamen's orders rang to the sky as they drew back their arms, and the waters boiled. Then they clove [tore] through the furrows [spaces between waves] with steady strokes and the whole sea was slashed by trident-prow and striving oar. No chariot drawn by a tandem team ever shot out from its starting gate with such a headlong thrust, nor charioteer . . . leaned forward so to the lash. Then the woodland rang with the cheers of men and the urgent appeals of eager supporters—and the high hills resounded and the sound rolled round the low line of the shore.[114]

Just as the Greeks and Romans raced boats as well as fought in them, they fished both for relaxation and for food.

In his piece about the resort region near Formiae, Martial depicts a man fishing near a house built right on the shoreline: "Not far the fisher needs to roam, but in the waters clear and still beneath the casement of his home may watch and take his prey at will; and here . . . the [dinner] table lacks not dainty fare; the fish-pool fears no angry wave; pike, mullet, lampreys, all are there."[115] Pliny describes a similar situation he enjoyed at a house he owned on Lake Como in northern Italy: "The waves break against the [house] and you can fish from it yourself, casting your line from your bedroom window and practically from your bed as if you were in a boat."[116]

Ancient Hunting

Like fishing, in ancient times hunting was both a means of securing food and a sport. Although some Greeks and Romans of average means probably hunted animals for sport, this pastime was normally associated with aristocrats and other wealthy individuals who could afford horses, hounds, teams of servants to carry supplies and dead

Madder than Ever to Win

Here are more excerpts from the long, thrilling boat race featured in book 5 of Virgil's immortal Aeneid *(Patric Dickinson's translation).*

"They made a supreme effort; the brazen keel shuddered under the pulse of their mighty strokes. The sea slipped under them. Their throats were parched, their lungs were almost bursting, their sweat poured off in streams. And a sheer chance brought to the heroes the honor they coveted; for Sergestus [one of the captains], in a fever of excitement, kept bearing in towards the rocks and thrusting on the inside berth [racing lane], with lessening room to maneuver, until he ran, by ill luck, onto a reef. The very rock shuddered; against the jagged edges of flint the oars splintered and broke; the prow hung high and dry. . . . Mnestheus [another captain] now was jubilant and madder than ever to win, and with the wind at his beck and call and his oarsmen striking a fast rate, he scudded over the open water landward. . . . In the *Pristis* now Mnestheus skimmed through the last lanes of water as the wake of the boat simply propelled her onward. Sergestus he left behind, still in the toils of the reef and shallows, calling in vain for help."

game, and so forth. "[Roman] landowners probably invited friends to stay over for a few days to enjoy hunting parties," Jo-Ann Shelton explains.

> Some hunting involved the pursuit of the hunted animal either by horseback or on foot. In other cases, the hunters did not track down their quarry, but simply waited in one spot while beaters with dogs drove the animals into nets. Once the animals were ensnared, the "hunters" stabbed them and then claimed to have made a kill.[117]

Pliny disapproved of this approach, thinking it dishonest and unsporting, and praised his friend, the emperor Trajan, for tracking his prey through the wilderness like a "real man."

Almost any animal was fair game for ancient hunters, although the most common kinds included wild boars, bears, foxes, deer, rabbits, and birds (birdhunting is referred to as fowling). A number of ancient writers described or offered advice about hunting specific species. Homer's *Odyssey*, for example, features an exciting boar hunt in which the beast gores the hero, Odysseus; and the fourth-century B.C. Greek general and historian Xenophon (pronounced ZEN-uh-phon) offered the following advice about bagging deer:

> If the trap catches the front leg of the deer, he will be taken quickly, for the trap will strike every part of his body and head as he tries to run. But if the trap catches a hind leg, the drag of the trap will also interfere with the whole body. Sometimes the clog [wooden stake to which the trap was attached] is caught in the fork of a tree, and unless

This fifth-century A.D. Roman mosaic (now in Paris's Louvre museum) shows mounted hunters spearing lions and tigers. More often, the prey consisted of foxes, deer, rabbits, and birds.

A Homeric Hero Versus a Wild Boar

This is the famous fight between Odysseus and the boar from Homer's Odyssey *(E. V. Rieu's translation).*

"Climbing the steep and wooded heights of Mt. Parnassus, they [the hunters] soon found themselves on the windswept folds of the mountain; and it was just as the Sun [i.e., the sun-god Helios] . . . was touching the plowlands with his first beams, that the beaters reached a certain wooded glen. The hounds, hot on the scent, preceded them. Behind came . . . good Odysseus, close up on the pack and swinging his long spear. It was at this spot that a mighty boar had its lair, in a thicket so dense that when the winds blew moist not a breath could get inside. . . . The boar heard the footfalls of the men and hounds as they pressed forward in the chase. He sallied out from his den and with bristling back and eyes aflame, he faced the hunters. Odysseus was the first to act. Poising his long spear in his great hand, he rushed in, eager to score a hit. But the boar was too quick and caught him above the knee, where he gave him a long flesh-wound with a cross lunge of his tusk, but failed to reach the bone. Odysseus's thrust went home as well. He struck him on the right shoulder, and the point of his bright spear transfixed [ran through] the boar, who sank to earth with a grunt and there gave up his life."

the cord breaks, the deer is captured then and there. But whether you overtake the deer in this way or wear the animal down, do not approach it, for if it is a stag it will gore you with its antlers or kick you. If it is a doe, it will kick.[118]

The hunting expeditions of the upper-class elite became especially popular in the fourth century A.D., an era in which a small number of Greek and Roman notables amassed truly enormous fortunes.[119] One of these men, the Roman politician and orator Quintus Symmachus, who owned nineteen houses and estates scattered throughout Italy, told a young friend:

I am delighted that your hunting has been so successful, that you can honor the gods and gratify your friends—the gods by nailing up antlers of stags and fangs of wild boars on the walls of their temples, your friends by sending them presents of game. . . . This is the right occupation for men of your age. Young men should relax from their studies

Mount Etna, a volcano in Sicily, was a favorite attraction for ancient mountaineers. Over time, enthusiasts constructed climbers' huts and lookouts similar to those found on mountain slopes today.

not in dicing, playing ball or trundling a hoop, but in exhausting spirited activity and in the enjoyment of exercising courage in a way that can do no harm. I shall encourage my boy to hunt as soon as he is old enough.[120]

Climbing Every Mountain?

Mountain climbing is another activity that, like hunting and fishing, is usually associated with the wilderness and getting back to nature. But *unlike* hunting and fishing,

climbing mountains for sport is apparently mostly a fairly recent development. Both Greece and Italy are mountainous countries; so their inhabitants had no choice but to learn to traverse rugged hillsides. Unlike modern mountaineers, however, it appears that few classical climbers did it out of any particular love of climbing. According to historian Waldo Sweet, the Greeks and the Romans had one thing in common, namely that

they considered the mountains an abominable mistake of nature. There was steady traffic over the Alps, but no one was inspired to comment on the beauty of the mountains. Very few ancients climbed a mountain "because it was there," as the modern cliché has it. If one did climb a peak, it was by the easiest route. There is no evidence that there were ascents where the climber deliberately chose the most difficult route.[121]

Thus, for instance, Philip V, king of the Greek kingdom of Macedonia in the early 200s B.C., climbed eight-thousand-foot Mt. Haimos (in what was then northern Macedonia and now Bulgaria) for practical reasons. It was rumored that from the summit one could see a vast panorama stretching from the Alps to the Black Sea; and he hoped that seeing it would help him to plan his coming campaign against the invading Romans. As the first-century B.C. Roman historian Livy tells it,

> At first the foothills presented only moderate difficulties; but as they reached the high levels they were increasingly faced with wooded and often impassible ground. . . . When they got near to the crest [summit], everything was so covered with mist . . . that they were slowed down as much as if they were on a night march. At last, on the third day, they reached the summit. . . . All of them were in a distressed condition, and especially the king himself, because of the difficulty of the route.[122]

Nevertheless, some evidence exists to suggest that at least a few people in classical times climbed mountains for the enjoyment of either the climb itself or the lovely view the summit provided. The first-century B.C. Greek traveler Strabo described mountains, including Sicily's famous Mt. Etna, which featured lookouts, huts with sleeping accommodations, and other facilities built expressly for the use of climbers. In one passage he seems to suggest that climbing Mt. Etna, an active volcano, was a regular tourist activity:

> Near the town of Centoripa is a small village called Etna, which takes in climbers and sends them on their way, for the ridge of the mountain begins here. Those who had recently climbed the summit told me that at the top was a level plain. . . . Two of their party were courageous enough to venture into the plain of this crater, but since the sand on which they were walking was becoming hotter and deeper, they turned back.[123]

However unusual sport mountaineering may have been in ancient times, stories like this one show that a sense of adventure and risk-taking is a universal trait shared by people in all lands and times.

The Decline of Classical Sports and Their Modern Revival

Between the fourth and seventh centuries A.D., classical civilization declined, disintegrated, and eventually gave way to the Christianized Europe of medieval times, also called the Middle Ages. Along with other aspects of Greek and Roman society, most traditional and widely popular sports and games disappeared, not to be rediscovered or revived for many centuries.

The Olympic Games, for instance, probably ended in the late fourth century, although the exact date of the last Olympic festival is unknown. In 393, the Roman emperor Theodosius I, an avid Christian, banned all pagan (non-Christian) religions;[124] yet some athletic contests may have continued at Olympia until circa 426, when Theodosius II ordered all pagan temples in the eastern Mediterranean, including Olympia's Temple of Zeus, burned. The last recorded Olympic victory was that of a boxer named Varazadates, who won in 385. Between the fifth and eighth centuries, successive waves of northern European invaders (the so-called barbarians who overran the Roman Empire) invaded the northern Peloponnesus, ransacking the remains of Olympia in the process. Earthquakes, floods, and land-slides finished the job in the centuries that followed; and in time the location of the long-famous site was forgotten.

In the meantime, Rome's popular sporting spectacles met a similar fate. Most

A marble bust of the Roman emperor Theodosius I (reigned A.D. 392-395), a Christian ruler who banned the worship of pagan gods, presumably including athletic contests held in their honor.

The Roman Colosseum today. The missing arena floor reveals some of the elaborate understructure, including cages for the animals and elevators to transport them to the surface.

Christians viewed the gladiatorial games as both murder and an offense against humanity. The second-century A.D. Christian apologist Tertullian harshly denounced arena spectators, saying,

> He who shudders at the body of a man who died by nature's law . . . will, in the amphitheater, gaze down with most tolerant eyes on the bodies of men mangled, torn to pieces, defiled with their own blood; yes, and he who comes to the spectacle to signify his approval of

murder being punished, will have a reluctant gladiator hounded on with lash and rod to do murder.[125]

Roman pagans wanted gladiatorial games to remain. But they eventually had to give way to the increasing power of the Christians, and perhaps about the year 440 the last gladiatorial fights took place in the Colosseum. The execution of criminals and beast hunts continued to be held for at least another century. But soon after this period the city of Rome rapidly declined, fell into disrepair, and became largely depopulated. By the end of the sixth century, grass had begun to grow on the Colosseum's deserted bleachers, where for so long great crowds had milled and cheered.

In the wake of Rome's decline and fall, the Great Circus and other Roman racetracks in the western Empire were also abandoned. However, chariot racing survived for several more centuries in the Empire's eastern sector, which became the Greek Byzantine Empire. It was in Constantinople's great racetrack in 532 that some 30,000 people died during the bloody Nika Revolt, ignited by disgruntled racing fans. In time, however, Byzantine racing declined as well, in large part because it became too expensive to stage in a realm that was itself in rapid decline. In 1453, the Ottoman Turks sacked Constantinople, eliminating the last remaining remnant of ancient Greek and Roman civilization.

Early Olympic Revivals

Many centuries passed. During these years the glories of ancient sport were largely a faint and distorted memory and few even considered reviving the games described in the surviving accounts of Pausanias and other long-dead writers. One who did was an Englishman named Robert Dover. In 1636 he organized a little-known, small-scale local athletic competition, loosely modeled on the ancient Olympics, that may have been held periodically until the early 1800s.

Others were inspired with the same idea in the century following the unexpected and momentous discovery of the site of ancient Olympia in 1766 (by Richard Chandler, an English collector of old relics). Over the course of several decades, archaeologists steadily uncovered the site, studied its remains, and began piecing together a picture of its once world-renowned ceremonies and games. In 1859, using funds supplied by a wealthy Greek who wanted to see his country revive the ancient Games, the Greek government staged a competition that included three footraces, some jumps, the discus and javelin throws, and a poleclimb (an early modern gymnastic event). But police broke up the badly organized games when many spectators became unruly.

In 1870 the Greeks made another, more successful attempt to revive the ancient Games. This one, staged in Athens's ancient Panathenaeic stadium, still only partially excavated at the time, added wrestling and a few other events to the 1859 program. According to David Young,

Athletes from all around the Greek world, as in antiquity, assembled in the stadium and contended, in orderly fashion . . . for Olympic victory. The winners were rewarded with their olive crowns and cash prizes, generally a hundred drachmas for each victor and fifty for second place. A large crowd of about 30,000 spectators looked on with great appreciation and perfect order.[126]

Coubertin and His "Gentlemen Amateurs"

It is no accident that these modern Greek Olympic efforts are virtually forgotten today. In the early 1890s, as part of an effort

Frenchman Pierre de Coubertin, pictured here, revived the Olympic Games in the late nineteenth century. However, the ideals that motivated him were British rather than Greek.

men. "The outsiders, artisans, mechanics, and such like troublesome persons can have no place found for them [in respectable sports competitions]. *To keep them out is a thing desirable on every account.*"[127] An American sportswriter, Caspar Whitney, who thought the United States should adopt the English amateur system, agreed. He referred to members of the working classes as the "great unwashed" and "vermin" and advocated keeping them as well as black people from "fraternizing" with society's "more *refined* elements," namely upper-class whites.

"Games for the *Elite*"

In shaping their vision for the modern Olympic movement, Coubertin, Whitney, and other elitists were much influenced by a group of classical scholars, mostly Englishmen, who suggested that ancient Greek athletes began as pure, "uncorrupted" amateurs. One of these scholars, John Mahaffy, almost single-handedly created this myth, writing that the contests at Olympia started out as "amateur performances . . . which were for centuries the glory and the pride of Greece." Professional athletics, by contrast, "was a rather low thing among the Greeks, who looked upon 'running for the pot [i.e. cash prizes]' with a highbred contempt."[128] Other scholars, including Percy Gardner and E. Norman Gardiner, perpetuated these distortions in their own highly influential writings. And they in turn inspired Coubertin in his attempt to fashion the modern Olympic Games as, in his own words, "games for the *elite:* an *elite* of contestants, few in number, but comprising

to reform France's physical education system, a French aristocrat, Baron Pierre de Coubertin, decided to create his own version of the ancient Olympics. But for a model he turned not to ancient Greece but to the athletic traditions of modern upper-class English boys' schools and private English athletic clubs. What appealed most to Coubertin about the English system was that it was restricted to members of the well-to-do, privileged classes, to "gentlemen amateurs" who competed mainly out of a spirit of social comradeship.

Most importantly, the English system kept out "inferior" members of the working classes. An 1880 article in a London newspaper, *The Times*, stated that amateur sports should not cater to working-class

A rare shot from the 1896 Olympic Games, showing the stadium in Athens filled to capacity. Contrary to later popular belief, this was not the first modern revival of the ancient games.

the champion athletes of the world; an *elite* of spectators, *sophisticated* people, diplomats, professors, generals, members of the institute." [129] To make his own Olympic vision a success, Coubertin suggested in his many widely read articles that he alone had conceived the idea of reviving the ancient Olympics; and he systematically suppressed the 1859 and 1870 Greek games by ignoring or belittling them.

The Greek Ideal Survives

Luckily for modern athletes, sports enthusiasts, and fair-minded people everywhere, the modern Olympic Games, first held in Athens in 1896, did not become the restrictive, elitist contests that its founder had intended. A few athletes did suffer from the Games' initial "amateurs only" restrictions. The most notable case was that of the phenomenally gifted American Indian track-and-field star, Jim Thorpe, who won both the ten-event decathlon and five-event pentathlon at the 1912 Olympics held in Stockholm, Sweden. In 1913 the International Olympic Committee (IOC) stripped him of his gold medals after discovering that he had earned fifteen dollars a week playing baseball in the summer of 1909.[130] For the most part, however, the modern Olympics have proved to be an even-handed and highly admirable sports venue. Athletes of every nationality, race, and social and economic class come together every four years to compete as equals; in the process they help to promote a spirit of international understanding and cooperation.

The Roman games and chariot races, by contrast, have not been revived, mainly because they were too violent and danger-ous. The exception is their re-creation in the movies, most notably the depictions of chariot racing in *Ben-Hur* (1959) and gladiators in *Spartacus* (1960). Hundreds of thousands of tourists annually visit the decaying ruins of the Colosseum and Circus Maximus, where long ago people and animals regularly suffered and died while enthusiastic crowds watched. The facts of these brutal games continue to evoke fascination, but also a healthy dose of horror, in the modern imagination.

Thus, it was the Greek, rather than the Roman, sports ideal that the modern international community has chosen to imitate, as exemplified in the modern Olympic motto—Faster, Higher, Stronger. The Olympic Games, the prestigious pinnacle of ancient sports, began in Greece in 776 B.C.; they returned there in 1896 and will do so again in 2004. The wheel has come full circle.

Notes

Introduction: Those of Whom the Poets Sing

1. David Sansone, *Greek Athletics and the Genesis of Sport.* Berkeley and Los Angeles: University of California Press, 1988, p. 77.

2. Sansone, *Greek Athletics*, p. 26.

3. For discussions of these and other theories for the beginnings of sports, the most comprehensive recent work is Sansone's *Greek Athletics and the Genesis of Sport* (see above). See also the prologue to Vera Olivova's *Sport and Games in the Ancient World.* New York: St. Martin's Press, 1984.

4. Quoted in Olivova, *Sport and Games*, p. 51.

5. When the Greek historian Herodotus visited Egypt in the fifth century B.C., he was astonished to find no organized games or athletics.

6. *Iliad* 23.362–72, trans. W. H. D. Rouse. New York: New American Library, 1950, p. 272.

7. Olivova, *Sport and Games*, p. 93.

8. A number of ancient writers, including Plato (in *Laws* 689), recorded variations of this adage.

9. The exception was large-scale chariot races, which continued for several more centuries in Constantinople, which had been Rome's eastern capital. See Epilogue.

10. *Pythian Odes* 10.24–29, in *The Odes of Pindar*, trans. C. M. Bowra. New York: Penguin Books, 1969, p. 22.

Chapter 1: For the Honor of Zeus: The Great Olympic Festival and Games

11. Quoted in Olivova, *Sport and Games*, p. 111.

12. By 500 B.C., almost three centuries after the traditionally accepted inception of the Olympic Games, about fifty sets of games occurred on a regular basis. Six centuries later (by about A.D. 100), the number of games had increased to over three hundred. The Greek "world," or those regions dominated by Greek cities, consisted of mainland Greece, the Aegean islands, the western coast of Asia Minor (what is now Turkey), some coastal regions of the Black Sea, southern Italy, and the island of Sicily. As Roman power expanded, it steadily absorbed the Greek lands (completely so by the mid–second century B.C.). Thereafter, some Romans competed alongside Greeks at the games, although most Romans much preferred their own, more violent gladiatorial combats to what they saw as "too tame" Greek athletics.

13. The prefix *pan* means "all." The Greeks referred to their homeland as Hellas (pronounced eh-LAHS) and to themselves as Hellenes, so that Hellenic means Greek.

14. Olivova, *Sport and Games*, p. 120.

15. M. I. Finley and H. W. Pleket, *The Olympic Games: The First Thousand Years.* New York: Viking Press, 1976, pp. 22–23.

16. Purple was the traditional color associated with royalty throughout ancient times.

17. The money collected from the fines was used to erect statues of Zeus (called Zanes, a dialect form of Zeus), each bearing an appropriate inscription. One warned that athletes must "win at Olympia with the speed of their feet and the strength of their bodies, not with money [i.e., bribes]."

18. *The Histories* 2.160, trans. Aubrey de Selincourt, rev. A. R. Burn. New York: Penguin Books, 1972, p. 194.

19. *Guide to Greece* 5.10.2, 5.11.1–9, in *Pausanias: Guide to Greece*, vol. 1, trans. Peter Levi.

New York: Penguin Books, 1971, pp. 222, 226–29.

20. This unpleasant situation was not alleviated until the second century A.D., when a rich Romanized Greek, Herodes Atticus, constructed a large fountain near the treasuries. A system of long channels connected the fountain to the faraway springs.

21. *Discourses* 16.23–29, quoted in Judith Swaddling, *The Ancient Olympic Games.* 1980. Reprint, Austin: University of Texas Press, 1996, p. 6.

22. *Guide* 5.24.9, Levi trans., vol. 2, p. 272.

23. *Guide* 5.13.9, Levi trans., vol. 2, p. 236.

24. The exception was the highly militaristic Sparta, where males began rigorous physical training (in preparation for war) as young boys. Spartan girls, who were expected to grow into tough, strong mothers and produce many males for the army, took part in many of the same athletics as the boys.

25. *Guide* 5.16.2–3, Levi trans., vol. 2, p. 245.

26. *The Peloponnesian War* 1.6.5, published as *The Landmark Thucydides: A Comprehensive Guide to the Peloponnesian War*, trans. Richard Crawley, ed. Robert B. Strassler. New York: Simon and Schuster, 1996, pp. 6–7.

27. Swaddling, *The Ancient Olympic Games*, p. 49.

28. Olivova, *Sport and Games*, p. 132.

29. Quoted in Waldo E. Sweet, ed., *Sport and Recreation in Ancient Greece: A Sourcebook with Translations*. New York: Oxford University Press, 1987, p. 120.

30. Quoted in Sweet, *Sport and Recreation in Ancient Greece*, p. 118, and Finley and Pleket, *The Olympic Games*, p. 124.

31. Quoted in Sweet, *Sport and Recreation in Ancient Greece*, p. 119.

32. *Pythian Odes* 8.83–88, Bowra trans., p. 236.

33. Robert B. Kebric, *Greek People*. Mountain View, CA: Mayfield, 1997, p. 68.

Chapter 2: The Glories of Physical Achievement: Running, Jumping, and Throwing

34. Scratching the starting line in the dirt gave rise to the term "starting from scratch."

35. According to legend, after carving out the Olympic sanctuary, Heracles had first set this distance by placing one foot in front of the other six hundred times; in an alternate tale, the *stade* was the distance that hero was able to run on a single breath.

36. The modern Olympics first featured a pentathlon consisting of the long jump, javelin, 200-meter dash, discus, and 1,500-meter run. There was (and remains) also a ten-event combination, the decathlon, consisting of the 100-meter dash, long jump, shot put, high jump, 400-meter dash, 110-meter hurdles, discus, pole vault, javelin, and 1,500-meter run. Because of the repetition of some events in the two combinations, the initial pentathlon was discontinued and replaced by one consisting of an 800-meter horse ride, fencing, pistol-shooting, a 300-meter swim, and a 4,000-meter run.

37. *Rhetoric* 1.5, quoted in Sweet, *Sport and Recreation in Ancient Greece*, p. 38.

38. *On Slander* 12, quoted in Sweet, *Sport and Recreation in Ancient Greece*, p. 28.

39. See Stephen G. Miller, "Turns and Lanes in the Ancient Stadium," *American Journal of Archaeology*, vol. 84, 1980, pp. 159–66, for evidence strongly supporting the existence of multiple turning posts.

40. *On Athletics* 8, quoted in Sweet, *Sport and Recreation in Ancient Greece*, p. 215. For a general overview of the Greek and Persian wars, including the Plataea battle, see Don Nardo, *The Battle of Marathon*. San Diego: Lucent Books, 1996. Excellent more comprehensive accounts include Peter Green, *The Greco-Persian Wars*. Berkeley and Los Angeles: University of California Press, 1996; and John Lazenby, *The Defense*

of Greece. Bloomington, IL: David Brown, 1993. The best general study of hoplite warfare is Victor D. Hanson, *The Western Way to War: Infantry Battle in Classical Greece*. New York: Oxford University Press, 1989.

41. *Guide* 1.30.2, Levi trans., vol. 1, pp. 88–89.

42. *On Athletics* 55, quoted in Sweet, *Sport and Recreation in Ancient Greece*, p. 228.

43. Kebric, *Greek People*, p. 77.

44. Phayllus was supposedly the only Italian Greek (Kroton was in southern Italy) who brought a warship to fight the Persians in the great sea battle of Salamis in 480 B.C.

45. *Iliad* 23.836–49, Rouse trans., pp. 280–81.

46. Having thrown the discus using both techniques, I agree with the second view, namely that ancient throwers used only a partial spin, if any. The more extensive modern spin imparts significantly more force to the throw, which seems to explain the large difference between the ancient and modern records. The best ancient throwers achieved distances of about twenty-nine meters or ninety-five feet, whereas modern athletes consistently throw over sixty-one meters or two hundred feet.

47. This is the same principle employed by a gun barrel's rifling, which imparts a spin to the bullet, increasing its accuracy. For more about the use of the *ankyle*, see H. A. Harris, *Sport in Greece and Rome*. Ithaca, NY: Cornell University Press, 1972, pp. 36–37.

48. Harris, *Sport*, p. 37.

Chapter 3: Muscle Mass and Raw Courage: The Grueling Athletic Combat Events

49. Lucillius, *Greek Anthology* 11.75, quoted in Sweet, *Sport and Recreation in Ancient Greece*, p. 71.

50. *On Athletics* 11, quoted in Sweet, *Sport and Recreation in Ancient Greece*, p. 216.

51. Michael B. Poliakoff, *Combat Sports in the Ancient World*. New Haven, CT: Yale University Press, 1987, pp. 94–95, 103.

52. Philo of Alexandria, *Every Good Man Is Free* 26, quoted in Poliakoff, *Combat Sports*, p. 10.

53. The term *palaestra* (from the Greek word *pale*, meaning wrestling) eventually also came to be used to describe a large sports complex with facilities for diverse athletic activities. The Roman writer Vitruvius provides a detailed description of such a complex in 5.11 of his *On Architecture*. See the two-volume translation by Frank Granger (Cambridge, MA: Harvard University Press, 1962).

54. Quoted in Poliakoff, *Combat Sports*, pp. 52–53.

55. See *Guide* 6.4.1–4, Levi trans., vol. 2, p. 295.

56. Poliakoff, *Combat Sports*, pp. 117–18.

57. *Guide* 6.14.6-7, Levi trans., vol. 2, p. 324.

58. Theocritus, *Idyll* 22, quoted in Sweet, *Sport and Recreation in Ancient Greece*, p. 79.

59. E. Norman Gardiner, *Athletics of the Ancient World*. London: Clarendon Press, 1930, p. 201.

60. *Aeneid* 5.404–405, trans. Patric Dickinson. New York: New American Library, 1961, pp. 105–106.

61. Olivova, *Sport and Games*, p. 143.

62. *Discourse* 28, quoted in Sweet, *Sport and Recreation in Ancient Greece*, p. 76.

63. *Pictures* 2.6, quoted in Sweet, *Sport and Recreation in Ancient Greece*, p. 85.

64. Quoted in *Guide* 6.15.5, Levi trans., vol. 2, p. 327.

65. Quoted in Sweet, *Sport and Recreation in Ancient Greece*, p. 150. Theogenes also won the long-distance run (*dolichos*) at a session of the games held at Argos in the northeastern Peloponnesus. This was an unusual, if not unique, achievement because then, as now, large muscular athletes did not often excel as runners.

Chapter 4: Bloodshed and Killing as Spectacle Sports: The Roman Games

66. D. C. Young, *The Olympic Myth of Greek Amateur Athletics.* Chicago: Ares, 1984, p. 173.

67. *Tusculan Disputations* 4.33.70, quoted in Harris, *Sport,* p. 53.

68. *Annals* 14.20, in *Tacitus: The Annals of Imperial Rome,* trans. Michael Grant. New York: Penguin, 1989, pp. 322–23.

69. *Satires* 10.79–80, in *Juvenal: The Sixteen Satires,* trans. Peter Green. New York: Penguin, 1974, p. 207.

70. In time some of these festivals lost much of their religious significance and came to be celebrated mainly as secular holidays.

71. The Etruscan homeland was centered north of Rome in the fertile region referred to then as Etruria and now as Tuscany. By the third century B.C. the Romans had conquered and absorbed the Etruscans, but Etruscan culture continued to influence Rome long afterward. T. J. Cornell's recent and masterful *The Beginnings of Rome: Italy and Rome from the Bronze Age to the Punic Wars (c. 1000–264 B.C.)* (New York: Routledge, 1995) contains much up-to-date information about the Etruscans and their relationship with Rome.

72. See *Caesar* 5.9, in *Fall of the Roman Republic: Six Lives by Plutarch,* trans. Rex Warner. New York: Penguin Books, 1972, p. 248.

73. *Julius Caesar* 10, in *The Twelve Caesars,* trans. Robert Graves, rev. Michael Grant. New York: Penguin, 1979, p. 17.

74. Quoted in Jo-Ann Shelton, ed., *As the Romans Did: A Sourcebook in Roman Social History.* New York: Oxford University Press, 1988, p. 345. For more about the remains of Pompeii, see *Pompeii: The Vanished City.* Alexandria, VA: Time-Life, 1992.

75. Quoted in Roland Auguet, *Cruelty and Civilization: The Roman Games.* London: Routledge, 1994, p. 53.

76. Lionel Casson, *Daily Life in Ancient Rome.* New York: American Heritage, 1975, pp. 100–101. The hunters were also called *venatores.* Some scholars suggest that there might have been a distinction between the two, the *venatores* being respectable paid volunteers and the *bestiarii* criminals or other disreputable characters.

77. Quoted in Peter Quennell, *The Colosseum.* New York: Newsweek Book Division, 1971, p. 139.

78. *Res gestae* 23, in Naphtali Lewis and Meyer Reinhold, eds., *Roman Civilization: Sourcebook II: The Empire.* New York: Harper and Row, 1966, p. 16.

79. *Moral Letters* 7, quoted in *The Stoic Philosophy of Seneca: Essays and Letters,* trans. Moses Hadas. New York: W. W. Norton, 1958, p. 172.

80. *Letters to His Friends* 7.1.3, quoted in Shelton, *As the Romans Did,* p. 347.

81. *Tusculan Disputations* 2.17.41, quoted in Carlin A. Barton, *The Sorrow of the Ancient Romans: The Gladiator and the Monster.* Princeton, NJ: Princeton University Press, 1993, p. 18.

82. Auguet, *Cruelty and Civilization,* p. 15.

83. Quoted in Shelton, *As the Romans Did,* p. 344.

Chapter 5: "He Came from Behind to Win": Horse and Chariot Racing

84. During these races, the story goes, he and the other Roman men, who had no women with whom to mate and populate the new city, kidnapped the Sabine women.

85. *Guide* 6.20.10–19, Levi trans., pp. 345–48.

86. See *Pythian Odes* 5.49–54, Bowra trans., pp. 183–84.

87. *Electra* 720–60, in *Sophocles: Electra and Other Plays,* trans. E. F. Watling. Baltimore: Penguin Books, 1953, p. 90.

88. Apparently Greeks from Sicily, where mule races were popular, introduced the event

to the Greek mainland. According to one theory, the Eleans viewed mules bred within their territory as cursed, presumably motivating them to lobby for the event's removal. This does not explain, however, why, feeling as they did about mules, they allowed its introduction in the first place.

89. On occasion an owner rode his own horses or chariot teams. Pindar congratulates one Herodotus of Thebes for doing so. And in the fifth century B.C., Damanon of Sparta and his son drove their own horses to sixty-eight victories in eight festivals.

90. *Greek Anthology* 13.16, quoted in Sweet, *Sport and Recreation in Ancient Greece*, p. 91.

91. Probably because the sport began among and remained under the control of aristocrats and other wealthy persons, they sometimes preferred driving their own teams. An extreme case was that of the flamboyant and controversial emperor Nero, who occasionally drove chariots in the Roman circus, as well as in Greek games, including those at Delphi and Isthmia.

92. Shelton, *As the Romans Did*, p. 359.

93. *Satires* 7.112–14, Green trans., p. 167.

94. *Epigrams* 10.74, quoted in *Martial: The Epigrams*, trans. James Michie. New York: Penguin Books, 1978, p. 148.

95. Quoted in Shelton, *As the Romans Did*, p. 356.

96. The other three were the Circus Flaminius (begun in the third century B.C.), the Circus of Caligula and Nero (first century A.D.), and the Circus of Maxentius (early fourth century A.D.).

97. Robert B. Kebric, *Roman People*. Mountain View, CA: Mayfield, 1997, p. 263.

98. Ovid, *Love Affairs* 3.2.1–84, quoted in Shelton, *As the Romans Did*, pp. 352–54.

99. The emperor Domitian established two more factions, the Golds and Purples, in the late first century; but they did not gain a popular following and soon disbanded.

100. *Letters* 9.6, in *The Letters of the Younger Pliny*, trans. Betty Radice. New York: Penguin Books, 1969, p. 236.

101. *Satires* 11.197–201, Green trans., pp. 233–34. In the Cannae battle, fought in southeastern Italy in 216 B.C., the great Carthaginian general Hannibal crushed a Roman army commanded by the consuls Varro and Paullus. Over fifty thousand Romans were killed. See Don Nardo, *The Punic Wars*. San Diego: Lucent Books, 1996.

102. *Poems* 23.323-424, quoted in Shelton, *As the Romans Did*, pp. 351–52.

Chapter 6: Of Balls, Beaches, Boats, and Bears: Leisure Sports and Games

103. 5.901–903, in Galen, *Selected Works*, trans. P. N. Singer. New York: Oxford University Press, 1997, pp. 299–300.

104. *Authorities on Banquets* 1.14f–15a, quoted in J. P. V. D. Balsdon, *Life and Leisure in Ancient Rome*. New York: McGraw-Hill, 1969, p. 164.

105. *Thesaurus* 9.104, quoted in Harris, *Sport*, p. 86.

106. For example, see *Epigrams* 7.72.10–11 and 12.82.3.

107. *Letters* 5.6.27, Radice trans., p. 141.

108. *Letters* 5.6.15, 2.17.10, Radice trans., pp. 141, 76.

109. *Letters* 9.33.3, Radice trans., p. 254.

110. *On Athletics* 58, quoted in Sweet, *Sport and Recreation in Ancient Greece*, p. 229.

111. Manilius, *On Astronomy* 5.420–26, quoted in Sweet, *Sport and Recreation in Ancient Greece*, p. 162.

112. *Epigrams* 10.30.11–13, trans. F. A. Wright, in Francis R. B. Godolphin, ed., *The Latin Poets*. New York: Modern Library, 1949, p. 594.

113. The Greeks must not have seen these as important events, for the prizes listed (three

hundred drachmas, two hundred free meals) were far smaller than those awarded in the footraces and other premiere events.

114. 5.134–50, Dickinson trans., pp. 97–98.

115. *Epigrams* 10.30.16–18, Wright trans., p. 595.

116. *Letters* 9.7.4, Radice trans., p. 237.

117. Shelton, *As the Romans Did*, p. 323.

118. *On Hunting* 9.19–20, quoted in Sweet, *Sport and Recreation in Ancient Greece*, p. 171.

119. As the Roman Empire's economy steadily deteriorated in these years, the political and financial clout of the towns declined and the rich and powerful, once mainly urban-dwelling absentee landlords, began withdrawing to their country estates. There, they often defied the tax collectors, made huge sums through land speculation, and in general lived like minor kings.

120. *Letters* 5.68, quoted in Balsdon, *Life and Leisure*, p. 220.

121. Sweet, *Sport and Recreation in Ancient Greece*, p. 155.

122. *The History of Rome from Its Foundation* 40.22, in *Livy: Rome and the Mediterranean*, trans. Henry Bettenson. New York: Penguin Books, 1976, pp. 461–62.

123. *Geography* 6.2.8, quoted in Sweet, *Sport and Recreation in Ancient Greece*, p. 158.

Epilogue: The Decline of Classical Sports and Their Modern Revival

124. Long a pagan society, Rome embraced Christianity in the fourth century, after the emperor Constantine I (reigned 307–337) granted its members religious toleration. In Theodosius's time, Christianity became the Empire's official faith. For an overview, see Chapter 4, "'Conquer by This': Constantine and the Triumph of Christianity," in Don Nardo, *The Decline and Fall of the Roman Empire*. San Diego: Lucent Books, 1998; for a more comprehensive treatment, see A. H. M. Jones, *Constantine and the Conversion of Europe*. Toronto: University of Toronto Press, 1978.

125. *Apology*, quoted in Quennell, *The Colosseum*, p. 75.

126. Young, *The Olympic Myth*, p. 31.

127. Quoted in Young, *The Olympic Myth*, p. 21.

128. Quoted in Young, *The Olympic Myth*, p. 45.

129. Quoted in Young, *The Olympic Myth*, p. 57.

130. After ignoring repeated pleas by many individuals and groups to restore Thorpe's medals and Olympic records, and long after his death (in 1953), in 1982 the IOC finally gave in. It presented replicas of his medals to surviving members of his family in January 1983. See Don Nardo, *The Importance of Jim Thorpe*. San Diego: Lucent Books, 1994.

For Further Reading

Author's Note: The following clearly written introductory books provide much useful background information about the Greek and Roman societies that sponsored ancient athletics, games, and spectacles.

Isaac Asimov, *The Greeks: A Great Adventure.* Boston: Houghton Mifflin, 1965.

———, *The Roman Empire.* Boston: Houghton Mifflin, 1967.

C.M. Bowra, *Classical Greece.* New York: Time-Life, 1965.

Anthony Marks and Graham Tingay, *The Romans.* London: Usborne, 1990.

Don Nardo, *Greek and Roman Theater.* San Diego: Lucent Books, 1995.

———, *Life in Ancient Greece.* San Diego: Lucent Books, 1996.

———, *Life in Ancient Rome.* San Diego: Lucent Books, 1996.

———, *The Parthenon.* San Diego: Lucent Books, 1999.

———, *The Roman Colosseum.* San Diego: Lucent Books, 1998.

Susan Peach and Anne Millard, *The Greeks.* London: Usborne, 1990.

Judith Simpson, *Ancient Greece.* New York: Time-Life, 1997.

———, *Ancient Rome.* New York: Time-Life, 1997.

Also, the *Iliad* and the *Odyssey*, Homer's classic epics, which this volume mentions frequently for their depictions of sporting events (the earliest known), are retold or discussed for young readers in the following fine volumes:

Peter Connolly, *The Legend of Odysseus.* New York: Oxford University Press, 1986.

Homer, *Odyssey.* Retold by Barbara L. Picard. 1952. Reprint, New York: Oxford University Press, 1996; and *Iliad.* Retold by Barbara L. Picard. 1960. Reprint, New York: Oxford University Press, 1996.

Don Nardo, *Greek and Roman Mythology.* San Diego: Lucent Books, 1998.

———, *Readings in Homer.* San Diego: Greenhaven Press, 1998.

Works Consulted

Ancient Sources

Author's Note: The most comprehensive general compilation of primary source documents about ancient Greek sports is Waldo E. Sweet, ed., *Sport and Recreation in Ancient Greece: A Sourcebook with Translations.* New York: Oxford University Press, 1987. Sweet includes quotes, many of them extensive, from the works of Homer, Herodotus, Strabo, Pindar, Philostratus, and Pausanias, to name only a few, and also provides much excellent background information and commentary.

Less comprehensive but still useful compilations of primary source quotes about Roman games and sports are found in Jo-Ann Shelton, ed., *As the Romans Did: A Sourcebook in Roman Social History.* New York: Oxford University Press, 1988; and Naphtali Lewis and Meyer Reinhold, eds., *Roman Civilization: Sourcebook II: The Empire.* New York: Harper and Row, 1966. In addition, the secondary works by J. P. V. D. Balsdon, H. A. Harris, Robert B. Kebric, and Carlin A. Barton (all cited below under Modern Sources) contain numerous English translations of excerpts from ancient writings about sports and games.

Other Translations of Ancient Works Consulted or Quoted

Galen, *Selected Works.* Trans. P. N. Singer. New York: Oxford University Press, 1997.

Francis R. B. Godolphin, ed., *The Latin Poets.* New York: Modern Library, 1949.

Herodotus, *The Histories.* Trans. Aubrey de Selincourt, rev. A. R. Burn. New York: Penguin Books, 1972.

Homer, *Iliad.* Trans. W. H. D. Rouse. New York: New American Library, 1950.

———, *Odyssey.* Trans. E. V. Rieu. Baltimore: Penguin Books, 1961.

Juvenal, *Satires,* published as *Juvenal: The Sixteen Satires.* Trans. Peter Green. New York: Penguin, 1974.

Livy, *The History of Rome from Its Foundation,* excerpted in *Livy: Rome and the Mediterranean.* Trans. Henry Bettenson. New York: Penguin Books, 1976.

Martial, *Epigrams,* excerpted in *Martial: The Epigrams.* Trans. James Michie. New York: Penguin Books, 1978.

Pausanias, *Guide to Greece,* in *Pausanias: Guide to Greece.* 2 vols. Trans. Peter Levi. New York: Penguin Books, 1971. *Note:* Books 5 and 6 of Pausanias's famous travelogue, contained in volume 2 of this set, comprise the most comprehensive single ancient source on ancient sports, including the most detailed description of Olympia, site of the original Olympic Games, and the traditions associated with it.

Pindar, *Pythian Odes,* published as *The Odes of Pindar.* Trans. C. M. Bowra. New York: Penguin Books, 1969.

Pliny the Younger, *Letters,* in *The Letters of the Younger Pliny.* Trans. Betty Radice. New York: Penguin Books, 1969.

Plutarch, *Parallel Lives,* excerpted in *Fall of the Roman Republic: Six Lives by Plutarch.* Trans. Rex Warner. New York: Penguin Books, 1972.

Seneca, *Moral Letters,* excerpted in *The Stoic Philosophy of Seneca: Essays and Letters.*

Trans. Moses Hadas. New York: W. W. Norton, 1958.

Sophocles, *Electra*, in *Sophocles: Electra and Other Plays*. Trans. E. F. Watling. Baltimore: Penguin Books, 1953.

Suetonius, *Lives of the Twelve Caesars*, published as *The Twelve Caesars*. Trans. Robert Graves, rev. Michael Grant. New York: Penguin, 1979.

Tacitus, *The Annals*, published as *Tacitus: The Annals of Imperial Rome*. Trans. Michael Grant. New York: Penguin, 1989.

Thucydides, *The Peloponnesian War*, published as *The Landmark Thucydides: A Comprehensive Guide to the Peloponnesian War*. Trans. Richard Crawley, ed. Robert B. Strassler. New York: Simon and Schuster, 1996.

Virgil, *Aeneid*. Trans. Patric Dickinson. New York: New American Library, 1961.

Vitruvius, *On Architecture*. 2 vols. Trans. Frank Granger. Cambridge, MA: Harvard University Press, 1962.

Modern Sources

Roland Auguet, *Cruelty and Civilization: The Roman Games*. London: Routledge, 1994. A commendable overview of Roman games, including gladiatorial combats, *naumachia* (staged sea battles), wild beast hunts, chariot races, circus factions, and the layout of circuses and amphitheaters.

J. P. V. D. Balsdon, *Life and Leisure in Ancient Rome*. New York: McGraw-Hill, 1969. This huge, detailed, and masterful volume by a highly respected historian is one of the best general studies of Roman life, customs, and traditions. In addition to sections on exercise, festivals, arena games, wild animal shows, chariot races, and Greek sports (as practiced by the Romans), it contains fulsome discussions of Roman theater, mimes and pantomimes, children's games, family life, schooling, slavery, dining habits, public baths, and more.

M. I. Finley and H. W. Pleket, *The Olympic Games: The First Thousand Years*. New York: Viking Press, 1976. The most detailed and in general most authoritative treatment of the ancient Olympics presently available. (However, it is out of print; if your local library does not have it, try inter-library loan, which might take several weeks, or ask Amazon Books, on the internet at amazon.com, to search for a used copy.)

E. Norman Gardiner, *Olympia, Its History and Remains*. London: Clarendon Press, 1925; and *Athletics of the Ancient World*. London: Clarendon Press, 1930. Gardiner's works, along with those of H. A. Harris (see below), are fulsome, detailed, in many ways authoritative, and were long considered the standard modern studies of sports in antiquity. They are still very valuable as general reference guides for scholars and devotees of ancient sports. However, Gardiner and Harris ascribed to the theory that Greek athletics was at first a "pure" amateur endeavor that steadily became "corrupted" by the "evils" of professionalism. This notion, which has since been effectively disproved by various scholars, most notably D. C. Young (see below), led Gardiner and Harris (and many others who used their texts as major sources for their own works about ancient sports) to make numerous unsupported statements and factual errors; therefore

Gardiner's and Harris's books must be read very carefully to separate the facts from the misconceptions.

Michael Grant, *The Gladiators*. New York: Delacorte Press, 1967. Although much information about Roman gladiatorial combats can be found in other books, notably those by Auguet, Balsdon (both see above), Barton, Carcopino, and Quennell (all see below), as well as various articles in classical journals, this book by Grant, one of the most prolific of modern classical historians, is the most comprehensive and readable general study of the subject.

H. A. Harris, *Greek Athletics and Athletes*. Bloomington: Indiana University Press, 1966; and *Sport in Greece and Rome*. Ithaca, NY: Cornell University Press, 1972. See citation for Gardiner, above.

J. H. Humphrey, *Roman Circuses: Arenas for Chariot Racing*. Berkeley and Los Angeles: University of California Press, 1986. This large, scholarly volume, the most comprehensive and up-to-date study of Roman racing available, will appeal mainly to specialists in and serious buffs of Roman history and culture.

Vera Olivova, *Sport and Games in the Ancient World*. New York: St. Martin's Press, 1984. This large, well-written volume begins with useful overviews of how experts think that sport originally evolved and athletic practices in the Near East and Egypt. The author then examines Greek sports, beginning with the Bronze Age and Homeric depictions, and concludes with Etruscan games and Roman festivals and games.

Michael B. Poliakoff, *Combat Sports in the Ancient World*. New Haven, CT: Yale University Press, 1987. Detailed, well-written, and well-documented, this is the definitive recent study of ancient wrestling, boxing, *pankration*, and other combat sports.

Judith Swaddling, *The Ancient Olympic Games*. 1980. Reprint, Austin: University of Texas Press, 1996. Though short (seventy-nine pages), this is an information-packed and very useful sketch of the ancient Olympics, including breakdowns of the day-to-day athletic programs and the dates when specific events were introduced, as well as numerous helpful photos, maps, and drawings. A commendable supplement to Finley and Pleket's more comprehensive volume (see above).

D. C. Young, *The Olympic Myth of Greek Amateur Athletics*. Chicago: Ares, 1984. This excellent volume, a good starting point for those interested in pursuing the subject of ancient sports, contains the most comprehensive and authoritative refutation of the old misconception that ancient Greek athletes began as amateurs.

Additional Modern Sources Consulted

Lesley Adkins and Roy A. Adkins, *Handbook to Life in Ancient Greece*. New York: Facts On File, 1997.

———, *Handbook to Life in Ancient Rome*. New York: Facts On File, 1994.

T. W. Africa, "Urban Violence in Imperial Rome," *Journal of Interdisciplinary History*, vol. 2, 1971.

A. J. Arieti, "Nudity in Greek Athletics," *Classical World*, vol. 68, 1975.

Paul G. Bahn, ed., *The Cambridge Illustrated History of Archaeology*. New York: Cambridge University Press, 1996.

Carlin A. Barton, *The Sorrow of the Ancient Romans: The Gladiator and the Monster*.

Princeton, NJ: Princeton University Press, 1993.

J. B. Bury, *History of the Later Roman Empire.* 2 vols. 1923. Reprint, New York: Dover, 1958.

Alan Cameron, *Circus Factions: Blues and Greens at Rome and Byzantium.* London: Clarendon Press, 1976.

Jerome Carcopino, *Daily Life in Ancient Rome: The People and the City at the Height of the Empire.* 1940. Reprint, New Haven, CT: Yale University Press, 1992.

Lionel Casson, *The Ancient Mariners.* New York: Macmillan, 1959.

———, *Daily Life in Ancient Rome.* New York: American Heritage, 1975.

F. R. Cowell, *Life in Ancient Rome.* New York: G. P. Putnam's Sons, 1961.

N. B. Crowther, "Weightlifting in Antiquity: Achievement and Training," *Greece and Rome,* vol. 24, 1977.

K. T. Frost, "Greek Boxing," *Journal of Hellenic Studies,* vol. 26, 1906.

E. Norman Gardiner, "The Method of Deciding the Pentathlon," *Journal of Hellenic Studies,* vol. 23, 1903.

Michael Grant, *The World of Rome.* New York: New American Library, 1960.

Edith Hamilton, *The Greek Way to Western Civilization.* New York: New American Library, 1942.

———, *The Roman Way to Western Civilization.* New York: W. W. Norton, 1932.

Harold Johnston, *The Private Life of the Romans.* New York: Cooper Square, 1973.

Robert B. Kebric, *Greek People.* Mountain View, CA: Mayfield, 1997.

———, *Roman People.* Mountain View, CA: Mayfield, 1997.

Otto Kiefer, *Sexual Life in Ancient Rome.* New York: Dorset Press, 1993.

Stephen G. Miller, "Turns and Lanes in the Ancient Stadium," *American Journal of Archaeology,* vol. 84, 1980.

Sarah B. Pomeroy, *Goddesses, Whores, Wives, and Slaves: Women in Classical Antiquity.* New York: Shocken Books, 1995.

Peter Quennell, *The Colosseum.* New York: Newsweek Book Division, 1971.

H. A. Sanders, "Swimming Among the Greeks and Romans," *Classical Journal,* vol. 20, 1924.

David Sansone, *Greek Athletics and the Genesis of Sport.* Berkeley and Los Angeles: University of California Press, 1988.

B. Spears, "A Perspective of the History of Women's Sport in Ancient Greece," *Journal of Sport History,* vol. 11, 1984.

R. Syme, "Scorpus the Charioteer," *American Journal of Ancient History,* vol. 2, 1977.

Waldo E. Sweet, "Protection of the Genitals in Greek Athletics," *Ancient World,* vol. 11, nos. 1, 2, 1985.

Index

Picture Credits

About the Author

Classical historian and award-winning writer Don Nardo has published many volumes about the ancient Greek and Roman world. These include general histories, such as *The Roman Empire* and *The Persian Empire;* war chronicles, such as *The Punic Wars* and *The Battle of Marathon;* cultural studies, such as *Life in Ancient Greece, The Parthenon, The Age of Augustus,* and *The Trial of Socrates*; and literary companions to the works of Homer and Sophocles. Mr. Nardo also writes screenplays and teleplays and composes music. He lives with his lovely wife, Christine, and dog, Bud, on Cape Cod, Massachusetts.